ONE MOUNTAIN, TWO MINDS

JONATHAN MEARNS

ONE MOUNTAIN, TWO MINDS

Printed in the United Kingdom
First Printing, 2022

ISBN-13: 978-1-7391262-0-9 (Paperback)
ISBN-13: 978-1-7391262-3-0 (eBook)

Print Layout, eBook formatting and cover design
Pankaj Runthala | manuscript2ebook.com

With thanks to the following amazing people:

To my co-writer: the incredible *Nancy Rue,*
without her this book would still be
a private jumble of scribble.

To my daughters: *Imogen and Arabella.*
Without them this story would have had
a very different ending.

To my fellow Rwenzori mountaineers:
Jake, George and Michiel.

To the *Rwenzori Trekking services*
and their incredibly determined staff.

To *all* who have unknowingly contributed
to my continuing journey.

And my thoughts are with all who were affected
by the Nairobi terror attack on January 15th, 2019.
And, of course, to Karen.

CONTENTS

PART 3 – YOUR JOURNEY

INTRODUCTION

It was finally over.

As we walked past the village school, the kids waved and cheered at the four of us as if we'd just returned from some great mission. Perhaps we had. Maybe we really did deserve that Nile beer we were headed for.

It was over. We'd done it. I'd done it. And it had been one hell of a journey.

As we arrived back at trekking services, I marched up to that front door where it had all started – back when I thought this was going to be just another climb. Just another story to tell after a cold beer. Or two.

But it wasn't an easy march. I didn't get much past the front door before I crashed on the worn, slightly springy, sunken sofa in the covered outdoor reception area and ordered those Nile beers. There were feedback forms to fill out, staff and porters to thank, and my jacket to bin – although I gave that to the kid who carried my bag all the way up and all the way down for something like five dollars a day. He was pleased as punch. The jacket had a few scars of its own and could tell its own story, which I didn't need to hear again.

The staff told us we were stronger than anyone they'd seen make the climb. They'd watched many people *not* make it, turn back under the conditions we'd encountered. Surely they told everyone that. As for the certificates, they were actually pretty cool and totally unexpected. We had indeed climbed a Rwenzori mountain – the highest in the range of eastern equatorial Africa. The isolated volcanoes Mount Kilimanjaro and Mount Kenya are taller, but Mount Stanley is among the Rwenzori the "Mountains of the Moon", and Margherita Peak is the queen of the range at 5,109 metres.

We had done it. I had done it.

And I was totally broken.

I had no fractured bones, though I admit there were moments in the course of those six days when I'd wished at least a leg or an ankle would go, just so I could be airlifted back to safety and comfort.

I was hot, sweating rivers. My legs were on fire. I smelled pretty bad. My face burned from the sun and the wind that had been bearing down on me in those long days in the wilderness. I never wanted to see another mountain again. As in, *never.*

I had done it, and *I* was completely done. I could have ended it all on that mountain, and when I say all, I mean all. No matter how many times I talk or write about this I can take myself to that moment on the mountain, and it's emotional. I can feel the tears gathering in my throat. I can feel my breathing change to something near panic. I can feel the cold seeing into my flesh. I can feel how close I was to dying.

Or thought I was. Clearly I was not, or you wouldn't be holding this book in your hands. Within twenty-four hours after my return, a different story emerged. *That* is the story I'm about to tell you.

However, this isn't just my story or that of the three men I climbed with. It's actually your story, whether you ever climb a physical mountain, a hill, a ladder, tackle your inbox or just manage the stresses that life presents. This is your story if:

You are facing problems – any at all – for which there seem to be no solutions in the foreseeable future. Your marriage or relationship is disintegrating before your eyes. You have a child with seemingly unfixable issues. Your job is pure hell or you have days at work in which you would actually rather *be* in hell. You're losing ground in some way, and you've pretty much given up on getting it back. You're wishing you could go to a quiet place and, when you reappear, it would all be okay.

Your life looks rather good to the casual observer – or even to the people close to you – but inside you are hopelessly watching your former dreams fade into what you now call reality. You feel the way a duck swims on a millpond: you look calm and serene while those legs are working ten to the dozen just to keep you afloat. You're living what nineteenth-century American author and naturalist Henry David Thoreau called a "life of quiet desperation".

You feel constrained. Struggling to find your path while worrying what others might think or say. You've read every self-help book, taken every 'get your life back' online course, joined a gym with great intentions and given up, stepped into every step-by-step programme – only to realize you have fallen into the old ways and you are back to square one.

You are at this very moment thinking: Okay, this guy is going to equate climbing a dangerous mountain and making it back down under the most adverse conditions to the metaphorical mountain of my life, right? Could it get any cheesier? That's what you're thinking, isn't it? Actually, I'm not going to do that. That was *my* experience. I want you to have your own adventure.

Here is what I *am* going to do. I'm going to tell you about my life when it was constricted with mental barriers. How, when I wrestled free, I recognized that many other people create mental barriers and say they can't do what they long to do. I'm going to show you how constriction kills life – and that there is no need to live like that. No matter what your circumstances, you do not have to remain stuck where you are. We all get mired in difficult and what may seem like desperate situations. We tackle them in the best way we know how, and that can have mixed results. We find excuses. The molehill grows. And before we know it, we are overwhelmed with the stresses. It doesn't have to be that way.

I've told this story you're about to read many times, and I've witnessed people take it and directly equate it to real life.

They've used it to deal with difficult people in the workplace.

People have applied it to deal with a vast and over-whelming inbox and in prioritizing their goals and objectives.

The story has given some the motivation to get up and do in small steps. Get motivated to go to and stay in the gym. Overcome being petrified of job interviews. Focus on personal development.

Basically, whatever your climb, at the the top of the mountain, the downhill is when it really counts – when you can be inwardly proud that you did it. If you are the literal adventurer, walker, hiker or climber, I'm sure you'll understand what I'm about to describe in this book. But no matter your background, this will make sense to you: we are all here to adapt and overcome.

I *am* going to take you through my journey from beginning to end – the physical climb and the mental, internal, emotional one. That's the only way you'll be able to make sense of what I'm offering. But then I want to take you through *your* journey.

I'll guide you in discovering your passion. It's stunning how many people have no idea they have such a thing burning within. In fact, some will even deny that life can deliver on a passion, so why bother. If you haven't figured it out by now, you probably don't have one, right? Not so. Its flame is flickering in there somewhere, perhaps licking at your physical being or creating a fire of resentment in your thinking. I didn't know my own passion until I came down from the mountain. As someone who has been through the mental and physical hell, I can be your guide.

I'll point the way to identifying your vision. I'm not re-ferring to the fantasies we all have to get us through the day. You know the ones: if you won the lottery or came into a mysterious inheritance, life would be so different. If you could find that dream partner, you could manage anything that came your way. If that ex-partner had a personality transplant and returned full of remorse, beg-ging for your forgiveness …

Not that vision. I mean envisioning the future in de-tail, from the climbing of the insurmountable mound of issues to the seeing of the possibilities from the top and back down to reality. A new reality. A true reality, where you are a New You, in charge of your own life.

When I returned from that trek up and down Mount Stanley and began to reflect on the experience, I made a startling discovery. I was a different person than I was the day I set out. I didn't originally take on that challenge because I thought I would find myself at the summit, nor did I take on that challenge so I could write a book. I was just going up a mountain because it was there, and I needed to take my mind off recent events.

Yet in the days and weeks that followed, as the burns, bruises and fatigue healed, something far deeper, emo-tionally deeper than I had ever expected or even knew existed, healed as well. I was far more aware of who I was and what I wanted for my life. And not just mine, but my daughters' – in fact for everyone I met who was as uncon-scious as I had been.

If you're still reading, you are one of those people. I want to give you the proper kit for your trek. I want to pose questions to challenge those constraints on your life – questions about the things you want that feel daunting, about the dreams you think are impossible to realize, and about the path you can take to get past dead-end answers and reach your own summit. Nothing is impossible. It just hasn't been possible *yet*.

You die once but you live every day. You have the opportunity to live and live big, to get out there and enjoy anything and everything. So I am setting this as my goal for this journey we'll take together. Imagine now standing at the top of a mountain as the sun beats down and a warm wind blows. You are taking slow but deliberate breaths through your nose. You are looking over a vast, open savannah with big blue skies. You take in the view. You close your eyes and breathe out through your mouth as you feel that heavy cloak lifting off your shoulders. As this happens, you raise your arms higher, tilt your head back and shout "YES!" at the top of your voice.

It is that liberation we will get to, giving you the inner strength to overcome anything.

How? By first telling you my story.

My journey up that mountain actually started just over a month before I even got to the start line, with a terrorist attack that took me to the heartbeat of life and the flatline of death.

I'll tell you how a day turned from a happy birthday celebration to working hour upon hour, day after day in the most emotionally challenging environment I have ever been in. And how a month later I was at the beginning of the mountain climb, hoping it would distract me from the death, the sadness, the wailing and the smells.

I'll take you through the highlights of the six-day trek, where the seeds of who I was to become were planted without my recognizing them. We will climb up . . . and we will come down together.

And finally, and most vitally, I will walk you through the application of those seeds – those principles – to your own life.

I began my journey with one mind and returned with another. That is what I want for you. So let us start at that beginning.

PART I

THE ATTACK

CHAPTER ONE
TERROR STRIKES

JANUARY 15, 2019, DID NOT BEGIN like any other day. This day started in an amazing way, an exquisite way. Weather-wise, it was lovely and hot, January being the middle of summer in Nairobi, Kenya. Personally, it was a day of light and joy in the moment – excitement and promise for the future.

I live and work in East Africa as a counterterrorist liaison officer, not in itself a typically light and joyful profession where you see the good life. Although, before you imagine too much of what you've seen in films starring fearless men and women who live on the edge of danger every minute, my role was (and is) basically to take my years of experience and, with others, jointly help in the counterterrorism effort. Unfortunately, this is a problem that isn't going away any time soon.

That morning, January 15, I was running a workshop at a hotel in Nairobi. During the breaks I stole moments to smile at the whacky musical videos my girlfriend Karen (name changed, to protect her privacy) texted me of her dancing around the flat. It was her birthday, and she was already celebrating in her usual life-is-for-loving mode. This beautiful Kenyan woman had helped me grow, and together we were truly a combined unit, bringing delight to each other's lives.

I had been married before, but that had failed some years earlier – not an uncommon occurrence – but I have two daughters from that relationship. Two beautiful young women who, when I lived in the UK, came to visit on weekends. It broke my heart to take them back home each time, knowing it would be two weeks before I would see them again. Every day, I missed them. I missed kissing them goodnight and telling them I loved them lots, just like jelly tots. I missed kissing them gently on their heads in the very early morning to say goodbye before I left for work. Those are moments I will never regain, but like many people I had learned to suck it up and move forward. I am clearly no angel, but I knew I was, and still am, a good dad to two amazing daughters I love to bits.

Still, the trauma of leaving their house for the final time before I went to Africa in 2016 haunted me. Even on the most special of days.

I travelled a great deal after locating in Kenya, and in 2017, just as on many other occasions, I boarded an aircraft to take me back into Nairobi. I said my usual hellos to the crew and walked down the aisle eager to find my seat and sink into oblivion for a little while. I counted the row numbers, looking ahead to row 10 where I had a window seat. In my place was a beautiful Kenyan lady. Beautiful. But she was in my seat.

I wanted that spot because physically I was feeling rough. The part of me that felt rough said, "I think you're in my seat." The part of me that saw how beautiful she was said, "But it's fine. I'll take this one."

She apologized and moved pretty swiftly. A bit of seat-shuffling and we were sorted. Now, I don't usually chat on planes, and I was especially eager not to on this flight. I had already decided before boarding that I wanted to sleep. I had picked up a chest infection, so I desperately just wanted to go into a veritable coma and wake up feeling rejuvenated. Turns out my new seating neighbour wanted to sleep too after a heavy weekend of partying.

Yes, well . . . we chatted for the entire flight, and not one ounce of sleeping was done. Our conversation, our connection, continued in the months to come. That was Karen.

All that to say, on January 15, 2019, I was revelling in her zany embrace of the day. Every video she sent me – and there were many – showed her dancing, laughing and having the private party *before* the party. She lit me up – as she did on a regular basis – and I was keeping an eye on the clock, wishing the workday away so I could join her. Our banter centred around our plans for a beautiful long weekend on a paradise island. I had noted the options, and I was planning to make the arrangements when I returned home that evening. There is no way to capture the happiness that shone off my phone screen. It was a joy to see Karen that way. A real joy.

Eight hours later, I was in the midst of another story. And it was not joyful.

Nothing suggested a crisis would occur that day. There had been historic violent terror attacks in this region, but nothing to suggest this was going to be one of those days. It was business as usual. Even when, at the end of the workshop I was leading, I received an alert of a possible robbery on the other side of the city, I wasn't concerned. There were alerts on a regular basis – some false, some real. It was part of living in that area. There was no cause for alarm.

And then there was.

At 3.20 p.m., the suspected robbery ticked up to a full-blown terrorist attack at the 14 Riverside Hotel on the other side of Nairobi from where I stood watching a far different kind of footage on my screen.

The 14 Riverside is not only a Western travellers' destination but a popular gathering place for local and international businesspeople. In my mind it is shaped something like a doughnut with the hotel itself in the central 'hole', while the ring around it houses businesses. The Secret Garden Restaurant hides in the middle of that hole and provides lunches, snacks and drinks in a pleasant – obviously, garden – atmosphere, like a small oasis in a busy, cosmopolitan city. It was there, in the Secret Garden at a peak time, that a suicide bomber detonated himself and the diners – who had no warning, no opportunity to flee.

With colleagues firing questions at me, I stared in stunned disbelief at the CCTV film of the bomber blew himself up. I'd been to bomb scenes before. I've been handed pieces of blown-up body and even commented in an almost jaded way on things like how heavy a leg was. Such is the dark place these situations put you in, and you find yourself making statements you never would have considered uttering before. Many times I'd seen the videos of hangings, stonings and beheadings, but there was something different this time. When you are part of a large team and an attack occurs, you know everyone has access to the necessary kit, yes, there is initially chaos, but the specialists know how to interpret every piece of information and how to bring order to that chaos. There, in Nairobi, we were a small group working with far fewer resources than we were accustomed to.

Yet it went beyond that, this reaction I was having. Being so close to where this heinous thing occurred and knowing I was to get even closer made it that much more disturbing. More atrociously real. I didn't realize it then, but that was the first sign this experience was not going to be passed off as part of the job.

In the confusion and panic that followed, three gunmen armed with AK-47s and grenades attacked the hotel itself, and that previously normal day erupted with a barrage of *ab*normal sounds: explosions, gunfire, terrified screams from the fleeing people, shouts from security forces. No one knew what was really going on, and no one could do anything but try to get people away from where the danger seemed to be coming from. That pandemonium, coupled with the absolute suddenness of the onslaught, gave no one time to protect themselves. Some did manage to escape, but most ran straight into the weapons pointed at them. The rest took cover in the businesses and the hotel, but to little avail. The attackers went through every building, systematically taking out everyone they found. Twenty-one people were killed – one British national, an American, the rest Kenyans.

I didn't rush to the scene. I had others I was responsible for, so first I had to make sure they and their families were safe and, if not, to be certain they would get themselves to safety. Once an attack goes down, there can be others. I had to take on a sort of fatherly role, which sometimes required firm instructions to get people out of harm's way. People, being people, said things like, "Oh it's all fine. I'm a few miles away, it's all fine." Well, maybe, but it's far better to be out of that shopping centre and back home – just for now. I had to make sure they were safe so I could focus on what needed to be done.

That accomplished, I left the training venue, which was in a hotel around the corner from the high commission, a few kilometres from the incident. There I set about gaining the information I needed to understand what was happening. There was a process to follow. I knew the requirements. Those were my focus. Under those kinds of circumstances, it's all business. There is no emotion. The emotion is saved, parked, either never to appear or to rock up when you don't want it to. Days later, having grown men cry on your shoulder about what they saw is sometimes a tricky moment.

The only thing we really knew by the time I left work at 3 a.m. the next day, January 16, was that the attackers were members of al-Shabaab, a militant terrorist organization. The struggle between Kenya and al-Shabaab had been going on for a decade over Nairobi's US-backed efforts to militarily defeat it in neighbouring Somalia. The timing of this particular attack remained a mystery. That was the information. Actual comprehension of that kind of full-on massacre is beyond most of us.

At 7 a.m. I moved to the next step, which was to go to the mortuary where the bodies of the victims were taken. More and more bodies were brought into the mortuary, mainly those who had been trying to flee but had been gunned down.

The mortuary itself was within view of the site of the attack, right across the road. As I arrived, the twenty-hour siege was only just then coming to an end. Some of those trapped in the hotel in the initial moments had hidden under stairs, in offices and in basement areas. We all know about the fight-or-flight instincts, but there is a third: freeze. A person doesn't know which one of those three he or she will do until they're in this situation. There is only prayer that whichever one you do saves your life. Although hours of firefighting led to the elimination of the gunmen, by then the terrorists had left no one alive. Shortly after, the lifeless forms of those who had huddled in terror all night were found.

I was intellectually aware of the situation when I made my way into the mortuary, but at that point, the horrific nature of the assault bombarded me on another level. Having been at the scenes of terror attacks before – I'd seen many dead bodies, each one etched in my mind, so I was expecting certain sights. I can recall key moments from those experiences – when hospital staff had tried in vain to save limbs, sometimes fingers with rings on them. On one occasion a lady had a facial burn pack removed by a nurse. As I watched, I felt like I was looking through the back of her face as clumps of skin and hair formed a pseudo one.

But a mortuary is a different thing altogether. It is a place for the dead, not those with any chance of surviving. Being surrounded by the deceased carries with it another level of coping. Mine was – and is – to believe I was looking at the vehicle of the soul which had left that body to go somewhere else – somewhere they or the family wished it to go. Each and every family there probably had a different view, but that had to be mine in order for me to manage myself as well.

Mid-January is the height of summer in Nairobi, with days of daily temperatures hovering around thirty degrees. This is a growing city of business, people and diesel cars, a city that from early to late has its high drum of noise and sensations, a city known for terrible traffic. The mortuary, with its large car park and gates staffed by security personnel (which is pretty standard at everything from mortuaries to shopping centres), is a prominent feature in that environment.

But there the Nairobi normalcy ended.

The day was hotter than the previous one, and the heat was intensified by the sheer number of vehicles. Once I made it through the main gates into the car park, I had to navigate the tangle of mtatus (small minibuses), private vehicles and emergency transports. Things grew more chaotic when I got out of my vehicle. A throbbing mass of people had descended on the scene.

Some were there to create order: a few individuals in white coats and an alarming number of police and guards all with the traditional AK-47 slung over their shoulders. Somewhere in the midst of it the press swamped everyone who would talk to them, eager for the story. These were largely local reporters. In spite of the magnitude of the attack, very little international coverage was done.

But most of those who streamed to the mortuary that day were members of the victims' families – pulsing, throbbing, terrified human beings desperate to see their loved ones' remains and horrified when they did. The side entrance to the mortuary – a place reserved on normal days for a few to sit – was crammed with a horde of screaming people clamouring to get inside.

The Red Cross had set up gazebos outside where they could help those reporting someone missing – those who still clung to hope – and took on the role of uniting them with their loved ones, alive or not. They did a superb job of offering support and on-the-spot counselling.

Many of those frightened people were unable to wait to go through the process that was being set up. Up to the metal back doors the relatives came in the hundreds, trying to force entry. It was a scene of deafening hysteria, but this door led to the viewing area and that was where these shocked, grieving people wanted to be. Soon, calm professionalism on the part of the staff would bring an end to that, but for a time, chaos reigned.

That chaos was not just on the outside. The reception area was separated from the mortuary itself by heavy metal doors, but beyond that, interior doors were non-existent. Large refrigerator units were pushed back, leaving space for the post-mortems. The deceased were on trolleys, available for people to see when they came to identify them. Most were largely uncovered, though some had sheets over them. In either case, those bodies were treated with utmost respect, with at least their faces covered until the staff bought the families in.

That was the best they could do to create some kind of calm under those circumstances.

You would expect a place for the deceased to be calm, quiet and almost peaceful, or at least that was my experience from previous occasions. The mortuary is usually a clinical, controlled environment with just a small number of people authorized to be in, whether that be police, technicians or whoever is deemed appropriate. There I experienced the opposite assault. My mind teemed with, *Hold on – this isn't right.* It was a mental jog – a mental shake to make me realize that whole thing was going to be different. I was a little disrupted, confused, maybe even dazed to be in that position, and the questions raced through my head. *Do I turn this way, that way? What's happening? If I do this, is it right? If I do that, is it wrong?*

The aforementioned police worked to keep the outside door shut, but somehow every now and again it was pried open and screams shot through the gap, as well as grasping arms and hands desperate to get in. I could not even imagine what was going on in their horrified minds.

All I could think was that if they all made it through in a rush, we would be in the stampede.

It was not what I was accustomed to, nor was it what I expected. But neither custom nor expectation had a place there. It was nearly an out-of-body experience. Was it really happening? Was I literally seeing bodies move past me? Was I really in Nairobi, post-terror attack? Only the overbearing heat assured me it was all too real.

I tried to look past that and focus on the amazing job being done by professionals without much in the way of the proper tools. I was proud of what the team was doing. It was hot, it was hard – and it was an important part of people's lives. It was the final time relatives were likely to see the soulless bodies of their loved ones.

Before I entered the area where the post-mortems were being performed, I put on a protective suit, overshoes and mask to prevent exposure to the teeming bacteria and the congealed body fluids. Even insulated, I could still smell the unmistakable odour – the mix of sweat, work and sticky blood. At one point, I was in the corridor near the embalming room, trying to guard myself from the revulsion as well as the physical hazards, when something squirted against the side of my face. I won't repeat what I said as it slid down.

It was an *Are you kidding me?* moment. The day had been a roller coaster of emotions, some of which I probably wasn't even processing. When I felt the jet of liquid, I looked up and saw the technician who was just cleaning down a body and prepping the next stage, syringe in hand. Was there a water fight going on? Did he really squirt that at me? Was it a dark joke? Whatever it was, I had had enough and I turned and walked. I didn't even have the brain power to ask or tell him to quit with the wild syringe firing. I still only hoped it was water.

Or maybe 'wish' is a better word. I wished none of it was happening. I wanted the blood to be water and the hope in the eyes of those rushing the gazebos to be grounded in reality. I longed for this to be a very bad dream I would suddenly wake up from, sweating and relieved. But it was the smell that assured me it was all too real. They used formaldehyde to clean, and even standing outside I felt like I had been sprayed with CS gas. Imagine being in a CS gas chamber, taking a deep breath before removing your mask just long enough for the CS to penetrate your eyes and nasal membranes before you put the mask back on. Well, the formaldehyde did the same.

A few times during the day I realized I needed to eat, even though the thought was repulsive. Just outside, but part of the same building, was a small roller shutter, behind which a couple of people were selling chapati, tea and samosas. It was there that some of the highly anxious people, seeing that I was in an official capacity, asked me about their loved ones. Giving them information of that kind was absolutely not for me to do. I was not to tell anyone of identifications, although by then I did know who we thought had been killed. That kind of restraint was agonizing – knowing but not being allowed to tell. I felt like I was stuffing down everything I felt.

Sometimes there *are* pockets of emotional greatness in those kinds of situations. I was with those injured during the 7/7 bombings in London, chatting to them. As I was going about it I came across many missing their loved ones, including one lady lying helplessly in bed. Unbeknown to both, the loved one was looking for her – neither knew each other were injured but, thankfully, alive. To be part of them being reunited was something very special, a moment I am sure they will treasure as they made a call home.

In the midst of the gruesome situation, joy found a place. I didn't stay close – that was a private call, and one I'm guessing would be full of emotion and tears of both joy and fear. I welled up myself, not just in empathy but in the assuredness that I had done absolutely the right thing. That is my most lasting memory of the 7/7 attack.

I was hoping for one of those moments that day in the Nairobi mortuary, but really, deep down, I knew it wasn't going to happen. The nightmare continued.

CHAPTER TWO

BLOOD, SWEAT AND TEARS

I WAS IN THAT MORTUARY for three days and spent one in the facility where the terrorists' bodies were being processed. I will admit to you that even now I am moved to tears thinking about that experience.

It's impossible to shake the images of all the deceased on trolleys. Twenty-one may not seem like a large number (although one person dead is too many), but the system was necessarily and wretchedly slow. In addition to the victims found dead on the site of the attack, the bodies of those who were taken to the hospital and didn't make it were continually being brought in by the police. Once inside, they had to be identified, and only then moved to the mortuary room for the post-mortems. None of this could be hurried which, accompanied by the emotional impact of each step, made the process seem interminable.

The rooms were teeming with people carrying out individual tasks. Those conducting post-mortems were like conductors leading their orchestras. They were in charge, it was at their pace. In addition, there were people putting clothes into evidence bags and taking forensic samples and official notes. Police photographers were snapping pictures. At times there were as many as sixty people in a space the size of a small nursery classroom. Perhaps even more disturbing than that, at least to me, were the university medical students bussed in to witness the post-mortems. It was right that they learned through observing, but this added to a room already packed with both bodies and professional staff doing their best. It made moving around the space similar to being on a busy train with standing room only and your stop is next but you are nowhere near the door.

Meanwhile, the attempts by family members to break through the back doors continued even after the identification system was established. Desperation seldom cares about control and rules.

Each morning of those three endless days of dealing with death, the professionals who were handling this almost overwhelming situation met to discuss what was working and what wasn't, in an effort not only to be more efficient and accurate, but to meet the needs of friends and family members who, unlike us, had never experienced trauma on this level and never imagined they would. Part of my role was to observe the benefits of the training provided.

I had that focus, but it was an eerie one, fraught with peaks and troughs. It was rewarding to be able to pass on information to the various embassies so they could notify their citizens, but deeply saddening to watch the faces of those who were learning that someone they loved was now gone. The only thing I can compare it to was being in a tunnel, the walls of which were the cacophony of noise, while the tunnel itself was as silent as a vacuum. When things seemed to be going fine as far as my role was concerned, I took those breaks I've mentioned – just to be sure it was all real. Those breaks took place only forty to fifty feet away from where death was being processed. It was impossible *not* to know it was real.

Most of the time, though, I was there when a family came in to identify someone whose death was still unreal to them. No one wakes up to the day, ready to go about their business, ever expecting they will end up in a mortuary that day seeing their loved ones. You expect towards the end of life that it's going to happen, but not to young, fit, happy people. Not one of those families ever expected it, yet it is what they will have to cope with forever. I found myself feeling that with them, imagining that person on the trolley was from my family, one of my kids. But I had to pull myself away from that kind of identification. This was their grief, their time, not mine. Each responded differently, but two are etched in my memory as if they happened yesterday. They are crystalline in my memory.

The first entered the three-sided room where the remains of their loved one lay on a trolley. There is always an initial silence in an identification as reality begins to sink in, but this family remained as still as stone. One or two slowly tiptoed around the body, staring at him with almost vacant eyes, but the rest were soundless. The voice inside of me, however, was screaming, Please, just cry – say goodbye – say 'I love you' – anything. Please! They did none of that. They simply left as softly as they had come, and the body was wheeled off for its post-mortem. It would later be taken into another room to be embalmed for preservation and sewn together with large, crude stitches.

Before you think I'm being critical, I'm not. My reaction, I think, was based on an experience of my own some years before. My grandad was suffering from cancer, had been for a while, and he was in hospital when a planned two-week holiday came up for my mum, dad and sisters. The journey of my grandfather's illness had been long, and they needed the time away. I stayed behind with him, watching as he became more and more frail. We are talking of an ex-Royal Air Force person here, a pipe smoker, moustache, who always seemed strong. He was a great craftsmen, always pottering in his shed. The smells of woodwork and pipe smoke were his.

He was struggling as I sat with him in hospital. He was not chatty, but still had a little time for a smile. The pain was excruciating, and there was only so far up the dosage of morphine could be turned. On one occasion while I was at his bedside, he leapt up, needing to go to the toilet, but there was no time to get him there. His robe snagged on the hospital bed rails as he started to wee. I tried to help with a small recycled grey waste pot. It was not a pretty sight. If he was embarrassed, or even if he cared, I couldn't tell. I couldn't even comprehend my strong grandad in such a sorry place.

One night during that period, I left him to make the forty-minute drive home to get some sleep. I hadn't been in bed long when the phone rang at almost midnight. The hospital staff thought it wise that I return as quickly as possible because my grandad had taken a sudden turn for the worse.

Crying and desperate that he not die alone, I raced there, probably breaking all laws and speed records. There wasn't even time to collect my gran. When I arrived I abandoned the car and ran in, past the reception counter with the staff and security gaping at me. I didn't care. I sprinted, sliding around the corners, to get to the square-windowed door of the ward. The corridors were quiet except for the occasional night shift nurse. Most patients were asleep and all visitors had gone home, just as I had. I knew I needed to compose myself so I didn't wake anyone.

When I got to the door of the ward, I looked through that square window and saw a nurse near the old wooden nurses station. When she looked at me, our gazes met, and in that moment her eyes told me what I needed to know. I choked back the lump in my throat as I pushed the old swing door open. She didn't say anything. Only the small shake of her head and her slight smile said, *I'm so sorry*.

With silent tears streaming, I followed her past the other sleeping patients, to a bed surrounded by a curtain. This was the last place I had seen my grandad alive

29

just a few hours before and now I was to pull back the curtain to see his lifeless body. As I held his forearm, his skin was still a little warm. I told him I loved him. I thanked him for the memories, the fun, the pocket money he gave me for dusting the daffodils and hoovering the patio.

I had missed being able to tell him all of that when he could hear me. By ten minutes.

Fast forward to the mortuary after the attack. With my eyes I was seeing a family I didn't know, but in my mind I was leaving my grandfather that night, not telling him the things I wanted to tell him, not assuring him I loved him, not saying that final goodbye. It had ached in me for a long time, and I didn't want that for these people.

The second family who continue to live in my mortuary memory were the direct opposite. As the first group was being ushered to the police to make their identification statement, this one burst into the room, clearly having been among those breaking through the back doors. They struggled through the staff members who were trying to hold them back and flew straight to the body. Rushing arms stretched out, wanting to hold, touch, feel, as if the body on the trolley before them was alive, about to do the same back to them. There must have been fifteen of them, though the sheer number wasn't the only reason the tiny area was suddenly exploding with noise.

Their grief overwhelmed not only them but those of us watching as they wailed and screamed – an outpouring of emotion I'm having a hard time describing. Granted, we British are not known for the full expression of our deepest feelings, and people in various cultures respond in their own distinct ways. Yet this running about the trolley, this full-out, untempered distress was huge by anyone's standards. I had never seen grief expressed quite like that. The high-pitched screaming sunk deep into me, so shrill it was bone-chilling.

Five minutes before, I'd been wishing someone would say something, anything. Now I wanted this heartrending scene to stop. What is it they say? Be careful what you wish for? It was a veritable roller coaster of deep, unbridled anguish. And it was to get worse.

I worked nearly 100 hours that week. During that time I checked in with Karen whenever I could snag a chance, making sure she was safe, but I didn't see her even when I took the rare hour here and there to sleep or grab whatever was available to eat. Finally, a week after the attack when all the bodies had been identified and undergone post-mortems, we were able to have dinner together.

We'd missed her birthday, and this wasn't intended to be a substitute. Coming out of the crisis and back into the 'normal' world was too surreal for a joyous celebration. At that point I was virtually living two lives – one in the day-to-day events that had gone on without me and which I needed to return to, and the other in a parallel existence of the attack's aftermath which I was still very much a part of. It was like coming home from the funeral of someone you dearly loved and wondering how everyone else could just be going about their business. Don't they know everything is different now? That thinking and smiling and breathing will never be the same?

Karen and I agreed that an Italian restaurant close to both of us which served okay food was a good choice. Neither of us was up to cooking, nor maybe even eating. What we really wanted was simply to see each other and reconnect. I felt out of step with our relationship, and I wanted to fall back in beside her.

At first, we talked about what I'd missed in her life in that week. She'd only been in a new job for four months, and I wanted to know how that was going. We moved from there to what I'd been experiencing. I couldn't share details, but I did explain the emotional elements, the highs and lows I've just told you about.

Karen listened with her whole self, as she always did, taking it in, strong mentally. She listened. She never judged. She just wanted to understand what I had seen, wanted to hear what it was like for me. She wanted to see *me.*

We had a deep rapport, we two, and that was evident then as her eyes caught mine and looked into my soul. I wanted to connect with her world, too, so I asked, "So how about you. How has your week been?"

It was actually a relief to ask a standard question like that after the week I had had. But was I expecting what came next? Not at all. Was I ready for it? Not at all. Karen looked at me from behind her glasses, her beautiful eyes welling up, tears starting to roll down her face. And then she said the words that sent the entire room sideways …

"I know what you mean. One of my friends was there."

I blinked at her. "There?" I said. "What do you mean, 'there'?"

"He died," she said. "He was hiding, and they found him."

Boom.

This was no longer something that was happening to other people, people I had only a professional connection with. This was happening to someone I loved.

Those words were like a truck, coming straight at me, hitting me head-on and leaving both of us physically shattered. We were together in that tunnel, where the restaurant noise and activity around us blurred and hardened, while Karen and I broke into sobbing pieces. At other tables, pasta was probably served and wine poured. At ours there was only the spinning of a surreal vortex, and my thoughts were at the mercy of that force.

There was me, caught up in my own professional world – pushing through the seriously long days on limited sleep and bad food. All that time, she had been suffering herself – a deep, personal grief.

And I missed it.

I didn't even know.

As I focused on her now, on what she was saying, on the emotion that was visibly tearing at her, I couldn't speak. I couldn't even see for the tears flooding my eyes. This – this loss – was something I did not want for her. Dealing with attacks myself was clearly not 'okay', but it was part of my job. I could always find ways to separate myself from that reality. There was no distancing myself from this reality, because it was her reality, the woman I loved.

It was no longer just 'part of my job'. And I didn't know how to deal with that.

CHAPTER THREE

A PLACE WITH A VIEW

I HAD A FEW HOURS OFF on Saturday evening during the events at the 14 Riverside, and I used it to go out alone to a restaurant that gave me a stellar view into Nairobi National Park, which is home to much of Kenya's wildlife. That may seem an odd choice given that the park – in the city – largely attracts visitors eager to explore forest and bush and valleys in the hope of seeing a noble rhino or the ungainly giraffes or a lion catching the sun. That wasn't why I chose it that evening.

I didn't want a busy bar – not that I haven't opted for one in the past after a crisis. I wanted isolation with a vista. I wanted time to allow my brain to catch up to the events I'd experienced for the last eleven days. I knew other people would be there, people aware of the recent attack but probably not directly affected, which was what I wanted. My life had been running at a breakneck pace, and I needed the energy of people just there to enjoy themselves. I wanted the bombardment of messaging, emailing and calling to stop while I gazed out over a vast expanse, where it would seem that nothing was happening.

Although there was a lot happening. Across the completely open land, beneath the acacia trees the aforementioned giraffes like to tuck into, the grasslands stretch. Off to my right were the Ngong Hills – peaks in a ridge along the Great Rift Valley. Their canvas of shades of green was still visible even in the shadows of dusk, and I watched as a small light aircraft almost lazily floated in to land at the local airport. The park itself, with its wide, broad savannah, is home to a large variety of animals: warthogs or a pack of pumbaa down on their haunches eating the bugs, the roaming wildebeest and zebras grazing. Hidden would be the lions, either relaxing in the shade or seeking their next meal. There's something calming in looking at this but not seeing what's hidden – all against the backdrop of the Nairobi city buildings.

I sat that evening as the sun was just easing its way down, imagining what was going on out there, unseen by the eye from that distance but vivid in my mind. Staring at that quiet splendour was for me like hearing the ting-ting sound of the car's brakes after a long ride. I wanted my thoughts to slow down, to eject the stresses just like those brakes getting back to normal temperature when the journey is done. My body was returning to its rhythm after nearly two weeks of constant intensity.

I had hope that my mind would begin to as well. It had been boiling feverishly in the midst of the crisis and its aftermath. I could feel the inner wretchedness, the sickness that came with images I would never be able to erase. I knew I was blanking out certain events, but I couldn't forget the holding back of tears, the demands on my focus and decision-making. Layered over that was my angst for Karen, whose heart had been shot just as painfully as the victims'. Seeing her grief created a grief of my own.

Now my mind could relax to a simmer, and it needed to. Fight and flight are good at the right time, but no one can withstand adrenalin pumping at its peak for too long before it affects health and mental processing. I couldn't do my job or help the woman I loved if I continued to be in inner turmoil.

I had experienced that at some level before. It's the nature of the work I do. But this time I was feeling a greater degree of helplessness. A heavier weight of responsibility. A deeper sense of isolation. As I pointed out earlier, in the UK I am part of a team of hundreds of people, and I can always find someone to bounce thoughts off, process the immensity of the task or just have a drink with. I had one great colleague in Kenya who fit that profile, but he needed time with his family. So I'd turned to the hills, where the sunset and the wildlife skittering about in my mind were slowly reconnecting me with normal life. I turned and I gazed.

And then my phone signalled a call.

As much as I wanted to ignore it, I pulled my mobile from my pocket and looked, gut sinking, at the screen. Another bomb had gone off in the central business district of Nairobi, and I was slammed straight back into crisis mode. I had to check to be sure my colleagues and

ONE MOUNTAIN, TWO MINDS

their families were safe. I had to get back to the city. I had to shake off the almost angry thought, "Give me a break!" Because in reality, it wasn't about me.

The attack turned out to be a small one resulting in limited injury and damage to property. Coming on the heels of the earlier traumatic assault, though, it was another emotional blow to Kenya, and to the people in Nairobi in particular.

And I was about to experience another emotional blow of my own.

About six weeks after the first attack, a co-worker asked me to check something out with him at the 14 Riverside. When I arrived – reluctantly – the Westlands district seemed to have returned to normal. The businesses in the "doughnut" were still cracking on, and although the Secret Garden and the hotel had not yet reopened, the foot traffic around it flowed as usual. The ability of the human spirit to overcome and regain normality is truly uncanny.

The same was not true inside the hotel.

It was of course far from ready for guests. The silence as we entered was eerie. Before the attack, the lobby and hallways were always teeming with activity – the staff welcoming guests to the hotel, the bellboys keen to get the luggage to the customers' rooms. Outdoors in their pool bar area, people would have been relaxing, taking the day off, holding informal business meetings, or just engaging in social catch-ups.

Now it was all unsettling in its stillness. There was nothing luxurious and inviting about the 14 Riverside as my colleague and I followed the footsteps of the terrorists who had worked their way through the building, looking for people to kill.

My imagination seemed to be the only thing that was alive. The disconcerting bullet holes in the walls and windows and metal lift doors popped like gunshot in my mind. Small stains on the floors where blood had not quite been cleaned up screamed at me in pain. Every step I took echoed the cruel footfalls of the shooters as I mentally and physically traced their path. It was as if I could see the staff and guests frantic to hide or running in panic as they were faced head-on by three armed gunmen.

But it was in a cold, grey stairwell to a fire exit that surreal turned to too-real. When my colleague opened the door to the space from the outside, I found myself in the place where six people had huddled all night before they were found and shot.

Every bone in my skeleton chilled to its marrow. I could feel their terror as they clutched each other. Their eyes were my eyes as they stared, horrified, up the concrete steps their killers came down to reach them, AK-47s at the ready. Inside my own heart the hope they'd clung to in the hours before – as they perhaps sent desperate texts and barely moved to escape detection – that hope died with theirs. What were they thinking as they took their final breaths? Were they trembling in disbelief, or frozen in the very worst kind of fear?

It was a frozen moment for *me*, that I know. Just like those innocent victims cornered in a stairwell at gunpoint, I could neither fight nor flee. My whole being was icing over. And I couldn't let that happen.

Yet I couldn't allow the alternative to happen either, and it does to some people in occupations like mine. After a prolonged state of high alertness and readiness, you would think a person would want a break to allow that pulsing energy to recede into a state of normalcy. But adrenalin can be as addictive as a drug. Once you've been on that high, you don't feel normal unless you continue to live at the peak, and no one can do that and stay healthy. Often people will talk about cancelling upcoming plans to get away on holiday because they feel an urgency to stay on the job, not even conscious that they're seeking the next surge. I always advise them to keep those plans, take that trip, go regroup. Or simply get back to a routine, reconnecting with friends and family.

Not that I always followed my own advice. I'd cancelled holidays and events in the past after attacks. But it so happened that, long before the crisis at the 14 Riverside took place, I'd booked a mountain climbing trip with some mates. It wasn't my first one – scaling the heights was something I'd enjoyed in the past. The climb was always fine even at high altitude, and as I hit the top I felt free, literally on top of the world with arms aloft – a truly liberating experience.

I briefly considered not going this time. I wasn't sure I was truly mentally ready. I was reluctant to leave Karen, who had been in her job for not many months. Her birthday had been rubbish; her friend had died – was this the time to leave her on her own? I personally was running on adrenalin and was not sure if heading off and out was the best thing to do. I'm not sure I had mentally tackled all I had experienced.

But taking the time off and sinking into my own thoughts in my flat would definitely not have been the right thing to do. It was Karen who encouraged me to go off and wished me the very best. She knew even better than I that being outside would be the best for me.

All right, so I should get away for a few weeks, breathe, do more of what I'd tried to do at the Nairobi Park. This would allow me to be totally remote, totally unconnected, with no mobile signal. Just the rawness and minimalist lifestyle of being outdoors.

I say all this to assure you that I didn't head for the Rwenzori on the Uganda–Congo border on a search to find myself or even to make sense of the profound effect the attack had had on me. The trip wasn't intended as a pilgrimage or a vision quest or a journey into my own soul. It had already been planned and simply came at the right time. I could climb. I could be free. I could see and feel the top without any worries. I just wanted to climb a mountain.

The mountain had other ideas.

PART II

THE CLIMB

CHAPTER FOUR

THE EARLY YEARS

WHY CLIMB A MOUNTAIN? If it was a good time to get away, why not a quiet beach where I could just relax on a lounger or where a hot or cold drink might be always at the ready?

I think the answer lies far back in my childhood, where most of our natural tendencies begin to take shape. Right now, imagine a young you freely going about your days, not a worry beyond the fact that normally the bedroom should be tidied or at least the bed needed making, or that you were being summoned for dinner when you were in the middle of something, and not being allowed to leave the table until it was all eaten.

You can still see your childhood friends, right? See them grinning. See short mental film clips playing back. I can easily replay the year the cub scouts were having a Christmas fancy dress party. I went as a cracker. My mum spent hours making it out of cardboard and crepe paper. It was a struggle just to walk, and that was made worse by the hundreds of staples holding the contraption together and tearing up my skin. Yeah, the fun times.

Perhaps you were sometimes taken to places on holiday, in which case someone else was always responsible for fishing out the suitcases from the wardrobe or the loft. As for clothes, someone told you the rules. The stuff put aside for holiday was for holiday, and under no circumstances to be worn out running around, lest they have to be washed again.

Among these scenes from your youthful past, you can probably also hear the voices. You know the ones, saying don't do that, don't touch that, stop doing this, why can't you just do ... Those voices stopped you from doing certain things, which saved you some pain but also stopped you from taking that step into the unknown, stopped you from feeling the fear and doing it anyway. I heard them – often – as a child, and I *wasn't* compelled to scale mountains in those days. Still, I always craved adventure.

As a young boy I loved nothing better than to be outside with friends. We played in the streets – practically unheard of today, yes? My mum probably labelled us as "rowdy", just to keep us in check. After all, we didn't want the neighbours thinking bad things. You can see what was happening – what happened to most of us as kids. The lines our parents gave us were to keep us under control.

I pushed that some. With cricket stumps chalked onto the wall, we kids had our game of cricket. It was overly simple, really, but we didn't think that. We used what we could find, and it worked for us. I was just out of sight of our house, so technically off-limits, but, again, I liked to test the limits. Even with my mum's voice nagging in my mind: if you get caught that far away from home, you are in big trouble.

A greater escapade involved a half-built bungalow. Most of its fifteen-feet walls were up, but the unfortunate owner died, and it just stood there, roofless. We saw it as an inviting building site. The land it sat on was heavily overgrown, full of brambles and rats. A wood-based tennis court stood rotting and unstable on the grounds, but it provided adventure nevertheless.

We made dens inside the walls of the ill-fated house with heavy concrete building blocks, creating entire scenarios, most of which involved danger to life and limb. Looking back, I realize our constructions weren't particularly well-built – we couldn't have been more than nine years old – but we managed to create those walls and, somehow, a pyramid-shaped roof that required heavy blocks to balance it just above our heads. This architectural disaster could have crashed around us but at the time our mantra was, "It'll be fine." What did we have to worry about?

Basically, most days I seemed to be out cycling, running and exploring all the sights and sounds I could get access to, with no thought to the potential mishaps. I felt fearless and immortal. I would go missing for ages and was typically welcomed home by shouting parents, pretending to be frantic because they didn't know my whereabouts. Actually, I believe they always knew I'd come home, grubbier than when I left the house and ravenous. I never was one to miss dinner. If I didn't get there on my own in a timely fashion, my dad went looking for me, and somehow he always knew where to find me. Funny thing, that.

If I'm honest, most of my excursions were without parental permission. I just sneaked out the back gate of the house under some pretext or just didn't say I was leaving at all, hoping that my absence would go unnoticed among the noise of the house. I must have been about six or so when my brother and I made one of those escapes – feeling like we were fleeing to victory. We devised a game that was simple and had basic rules. First, find a massive hill. Next, collect a sharp, javelin-like stick. Finally, stand on opposite sides of the hill and blindly throw the stick in an attempt to hit the other brother. Once your stick was hurled, your job was to dodge the javelin coming at you with just a nanosecond of notice. Easy.

Let me just add some perspective. The hill was certainly no more than a small mound, and this javelin-sized stick was probably less than a foot long, though sharp. A great game, no doubt invented by me. It was working pretty well until ... you can likely see where this is going. At one point the stick I threw hit my brother square in the face. Bleeding usually did have a way of cutting a game short.

We arrived home to find an irate mother who thought we had both been kidnapped. She was furious. When she saw that I'd managed to deface my brother, she went beyond irate, and we were dispatched to our rooms. Whether she tended to his wounds, I don't remember. What I do recall is that she'd even been to the local pub looking for us. Perhaps she was seeing into my future? My mother was never really a fan of pubs, and she'd definitely never been into one on her own. If we bring up this story today, almost forty years later, she still threatens to throttle us both.

As I got a little older, my thrill-seeking escalated. I continued slipping out the back gate and cycling with my mates – or 'borrowing' their bikes. We spent a great deal of time in the woods trying to get a Grifter bike airborne. For those who have no idea what a Grifter is, it's a robust bike, seemingly weighing about a ton – well, to me. All the cool kids had BMX bikes that seemed to go airborne with just a little help, but a Grifter? It was like trying to get a tank into the air.

We had a system, though, that we thought was in-fallible. On the Grifter at high speed (all right, it seemed like a high speed to us), all we had to do was approach a tree root slightly raised from ground level. When the rider hit the root, he yanked on the handlebars, hoping his strength, the speed and the angle of the hit would take him airborne. The truth is, any air we got seemed like six feet off the ground to us, when in reality it was more like a centimetre, if that, and for a nanosecond.

No matter what mini adventure I was on, I was always given a time to be home, whether it was the standing 'curfew' or one particular to that day. Rarely did I make it. I often pretended I'd been in the garden or the garage when it was time to be home, so that technically I wasn't late. I had good reason, I thought, to be out of the house as much as possible. If I was home, that meant I was doing homework or just bored. How does that even compare to being out exploring?

As tame as all that actually sounds, it was the precursor for my later philosophy. I wanted to slide into my coffin shouting, "Yee-haw! What a ride!" He who dies with the most stories, wins, right? My mother never did, and still doesn't, concur. She was protective of the four of us; an instinct that arose from her own childhood experiences. The one thing she bellowed at me constantly in my growing-up years was: "You and your hare-brained ideas! Why can't you just be normal?" It will come as no surprise that, given what I do for a living, she still says that to me now.

That didn't fall on deaf ears, though. While I seem to have been born with a sense of adventure, with a spirit that was always going to motivate me to get out there and do things, I didn't realize until my adulthood that her words planted limiting beliefs inside my mind. Those are the beliefs that have tried to wrestle down my daring ideas and my beyond-normal dreams. We all have those inhibiting voices in our heads, whether they were planted by parents or siblings or teachers or threatening life experiences or losses. We can probably name the times when they held us back. We're going to talk more about those later.

My adventures took a more organized – and sanctioned – turn when I became involved in the Cubs and Scouts. There I was taught self-discipline and respect, and I was given the tools to look after myself. All that took place against the backdrop of being outside, camping, climbing, night hiking and making temporary furniture out of wood found on the forest floor. I have to say, though, and this may surprise you, my favourite activity in the Scouts was outdoor cooking. I loved cooking over an open fire and, if you'll allow me a little self-promotion, I served up some amazing meals. We are talking starters, main courses, desserts (which included my specialty: plum pudding). My group won district and county competitions with me as chef and, later, as a patrol leader.

I was still into derring-do. It wasn't uncommon for us to build rafts from wood found in the forest lashed together with some large water containers. Or get pushed in a canoe or kayak into a fifteen-feet drop and enter the water canoe nose- and head-first. I was, shall we say, a bit spontaneous and sometimes not as well prepared as I could have been for these feats, but scouting taught me to dig deep at the key moments and pull myself through. It wasn't always pretty, but I always finished. Usually I went home after a week or so away wearing the same clothes I'd had on for a week, much to my mum's dismay. My view was that I was helping by not giving her so much washing to do.

If it sounds like I was a tough little guy, I'm creating the wrong impression. As a school kid I was this skinny boy with a great mop of ginger hair, either cut by my mum or the barber. The end result looked as if they had placed a bowl on my head and cut round it. Pictures of my brothers and me in those days are amusing to visitors as my mum proudly displays them for all to see.

I was a quiet, bullied kid in secondary school and not a terribly good student. I relished adventure but not schoolwork, which was never as fast-moving or interesting as I wanted. However, I wasn't the worst pupil either, because my upbringing taught me that keeping out of trouble was always the right thing to do. As much as I wanted to be out of that classroom, I did that 'right thing' and was mortified if I got caught doing something slightly wrong where school was concerned. The conflict in me was constant. The limiting belief, again, won.

Now I know that sometimes getting things wrong is the right thing to do, but if it stops you from even having a go, that's a limiting belief. I'm sure there isn't one of you reading this right now who can't identify an interior conflict you experienced in your formative years, between 'the right thing' and what you wanted to explore, test, experiment with to see if it really was right – for you. More on this later.

By the time I was a teenager, the gap between who I was and what was expected widened. As the oldest of four, it seemed the expectations placed on me were more than for my younger siblings, which exacerbated the constant tension within. Don't get me wrong, my parents were great, and they absolutely did what they thought was right at the time, according to what they believed was best for us. The older I got, however, the more aware I became that they had a different outlook on life than I did. That is, of course, an expected thing, but at the time I felt caged, desperate to break into the world with ideas and visions but suppressed by the ideal of living a quiet, 'normal' life and being encouraged to settle down.

I left home at age seventeen and joined a year of adventure with the police cadets. It was a programme that combined fitness, law and community service work. It got me into the best shape of my life to that point and pushed me to new limits by providing fresh challenges. It was as if the entire thing was designed specifically for me. My community service led me to working with the elderly and later with special needs kids, broadening my view of the world. I still have my project and photos of those lovely, elderly people, including when I took a man who had survived three strokes out to the park. He loved it, and so did I. I became a long-distance runner and enjoyed the mental freedom that brings. I was still by comparison nowhere near the strongest or the fastest, yet I was always up near the top, even taking home a few trophies.

But I think one of the most profound things I learned in my time as a youngster was that I was afraid of heights. Yeah, a total wreck, jumping off the top diving board, heading up mountains and, even worse, abseiling down. For those not acquainted with abseiling, just picture yourself at the top of a rock face holding on to a rope that is perpendicular to the rock and backing all the way to the ground. I had no idea until then that I had that fear, and there was nothing to do but defeat it. I didn't know how, so I just muddled through.

Everything I've just revealed about my young self surfaced in the adventure I was about to embark on in the Rwenzori. That includes the spirit of risk-taking, the childhood wounds and the self-limiting beliefs implanted without my even knowing it.

As I prepared for the climb, I wasn't thinking about any of that. And that made the experience more of a risk than I ever imagined.

CHAPTER FIVE

WHAT HAD WE SIGNED UP FOR?

LET ME BEGIN THIS CHAPTER about preparation for the Rwenzori climb by saying that on a scale of 1 to 10 (1 being *There's no point in turning up; I should just give my place to someone else,* and 10 being *Take a six-week leave of absence from your job and train hard*), I was probably sitting at about a 6. You know, fairly fit but not in top form.

While I have always been a go-getter, a doer, I seem to like the last-minute emergency scenario when the adrenalin is pumping and the heart rate is elevated. I do train; I would be an idiot not to. But there's something exciting to me about not being *completely* fit when I turn up for an event. It makes me wonder if my school reports said, *Jonathan has great potential. If only he concentrated ...* It's not about being lazy. I think the lack of full-on readiness comes from the fact that I'm seldom there to win or do a storming time. I just want to enjoy the experience at a respectable pace. It is, in fact, what I look to do through life as a whole these days. More on that later.

If I *am* going to do any disciplined training, I have to be externally motivated. This I learned during my time with the police cadets. On the physical side, the programme was military in approach. People were shouting at us constantly – for motivation, of course. *Get up that rope! Get over that wall!* Because in my adult world I don't have drill instructors perennially giving me orders, when I want to get out and do something physically strenuous, I re-enact that voice in my head. I rely on mental strength.

Have there been times when I set myself on a training schedule? Sure. When the London Marathon was coming up, I created a running plan and actually stuck to it for a while ... until it faded off ... Did that stop me from participating? It did not, and I finished. As I say, not record-breaking, but getting round in about four hours and twenty minutes. Yes, there were quicker runners and, yes, there were slower ones, but I raised money for a PTSD charity, and I had an awesome time in the people-lined streets of London. When you run that marathon, every single spectator is cheering you on from start to finish and even handing out small, sweet snacks to keep you going. Could I have done it in less time if I'd stayed with my ambitious regime? Who knows? But I had a great experience and contributed to a great cause, and that was my true goal.

Using this same mental method, I've managed to:
- Navigate the Ten Tors, a fifty-two-mile race, in thirty-six hours across Dartmoor with full kit

- Walk the UK Three Peaks Challenge in under twenty-four hours (Ben Nevis in Scotland, Scafell in England and Snowdon in North Wales)
- Tackle Snowdon across the Crib Goch Ridge. (I have to mention that when you are afraid of heights this is an actual feat. With the sheer drops either side and the narrow ridge ... I clung dearly to that rock.)
- Complete a fifty-two-mile run from Caldbeck to Cartmell across the Lake District
- Participate in a 250-mile bike ride from Paris to Platt to raise money for a girls' school
- Finish the London Marathon twice
- Finish the Mount Kilimanjaro Marathon
- Attempt to climb Mont Blanc, only to be scuppered by seriously bad weather. Fortunately, we came off the mountain; others did not and one was killed. I will return under safer conditions.

Fast forward to living in Kenya. In 2018, a four-man team headed up Mount Kenya's Lenana Peak, which is a 4,985-metre climb (16,355 feet). Two guys from that venture – myself included – decided the Rwenzori mountain range would be a great idea the following year. I had never heard of the place, but it sounded exciting, so why not? Part of the enticement was the information I was given that the peak we would reach was the only snow-capped mountain on the equator. That turned out to be less than correct, but it was close, and I wasn't about to split hairs. I was already in.

You may be as much in the dark as I was about this place, so perhaps a little background will give you some context.

The Rwenzori range is in Uganda, a landlocked country in the East Africa community, named the Pearl of Africa by Winston Churchill during his visit in 1908. It's the home of two UNESCO World Heritage Sites: the Bwindi impenetrable forest, famous for its gorilla communities, and the Rwenzori mountain range. It is the source of the River Nile. While, as I mentioned, Uganda is landlocked, there is no lack of water, as it sits in the Great Lakes region of East Africa. These lakes are reported to make up 25 per cent of the earth's unfrozen fresh water.

As for the Rwenzori, the range covers over 1,000 square kilometres and is home to Africa's third highest peak, Margherita, and its twin, Stanley. It is seventy-five miles long, marking the Uganda–Congo border and creating a strong, healthy barrier between the Ugandan side where, politically, things are peaceful, and the Democratic Republic of the Congo side, which is armed with militia and dotted with no-go areas. This majestic range is also known as the Mountains of the Moon, which may come from the first time the snow-capped peaks were seen only from afar and looked quite lunar to those ancient observers.

Impressive, yes? Still, in my usual fashion, I did just enough physical preparation. How hard could it be? As the date for our departure grew closer, however, I found myself wondering if this trip might be ill-fated – if perhaps I shouldn't go after all, despite Karen's encouragement.

The thought that I might end up as a posthumous star in a disaster movie entered my mind more than once. And *that* was not typical for me at all.

Looking back, I realize there were also concrete signs that maybe this wasn't a good idea. The slight doubts themselves bore looking at, but I didn't. There was a hassle with procuring the visa. And then, of course, I received a warning email from the company which was organizing the climb. Every such company provides that kind of "participate at your own risk" statement, but this one was particularly daunting:

Trekking in the Rwenzori Mountains is tough, much tougher than Kilimanjaro or Mt Kenya. Therefore, you should be fit. The eight-day trip is recommended for most people of average fitness and climbing ability. However, there are people who can do the trek in seven days, hence this seven-day trek. But be warned: you must be fit to do it in seven days.

That last line – *you must be fit* – was going to require some inner strength, some guts, some determination. Some digging deep. Because physically, I knew I wasn't totally in the best physical shape. Of *course* we had plumped for the seven-day option, which was probably crazy. Yet, even with the company-issued warning, I lacked complete comprehension of the size of the task ahead. It was a mountain, yes. It was high, yes. But I'd been up a few before, so, again, how hard could it be? Even when it was explained to me that we were to reach the equivalent of seventeen Eiffel Towers or thirteen Empire State Buildings or sixteen London Shards in those seven days, that still sounded relatively easy.

Especially in good weather.

We'd chosen that particular week specifically because we saw that clear skies were typical for that time of year. We had seen the iconic YouTube footage of the route up and the summit, which showed amazing, liberating views in that season. Despite any physical misgivings, I knew that mentally I needed those views.

So the warning signposts were clearly planted, and I chose to ignore them. I know now that when you make a decision about something with high risks, it pays to look at those indications that caution might be prudent. There is a fine line between doing everything that's high-risk, putting yourself in harm's way unnecessarily – and not doing something simply because you're afraid of things that, in all honestly, probably won't happen. I've found that on the other side of fear is life.

I did prepare myself in some significant ways. As I've said, I'm not a complete moron.

A seven-day trek meant we would be climbing faster than usual, and I knew it is not advisable to climb more than 500 metres per day, lest you fall prey to altitude sickness, which is nothing to be sniffed at: it can kill. I prepped to stay fully hydrated throughout the trek and reminded myself not to be reluctant to raise concerns if I began to experience the symptoms up there: headache, fatigue, racing heartbeat, nausea and vomiting, dizziness, confusion, shortness of breath even with mild exertion and difficulty walking in a straight line. When you have trouble maintaining consciousness and you're coughing up blood, you've waited far too long to say something.

Some climbers talk about medication you can take that either convinces you that you don't have altitude sickness so you can continue, or, supposedly, stop you from developing it at all. Neither made any sense to me, so no such tablets were packed in my kit. If I am suffering from altitude sickness, I want to know, rather than mask the symptoms. Sooner or later you'll succumb if you don't know what's going on with your body, that amazing creation that tells you what it needs. Checking in with each other and getting to a lower altitude if necessary were the only remedies I would be using.

I also felt prepared with the necessary skills. Margherita Peak is a technical climb, which means it requires knowledge of using ropes, crampons, belays and an ice axe (particularly helpful when climbing sixty-degree glaciers). My Boy Scouts training would surely kick in. After all, what knowledge could I have lost in the thirty-odd years since I had last climbed a rock face while attached to a rope? In hindsight, I realize this is where I stepped just a bit over that fine line into the unnecessary risk category.

I was feeling rather good about my kit as well. I purchased a four-season sleeping bag, having used the two-season variety camping on the Mount Kenya climb, which was nowhere near suitable. Constantly waking up cold plummeted my body past the point where I was enjoying sleeping at all. Getting good, restorative rest is crucial to your mental and physical effectiveness on a climb; tiredness will make you grouchy. For this trip, I had good mountain clothing, strong and well-worn-in boots, and I followed the kit list the company provided. Crampons and hard hats were available to hire at the site, which suited me.

I practised two sort of ritual preparations that may be unique to me. One, I avoided alcohol for some weeks to give my body the best chance in the high altitude. If I was going to fall, it wouldn't be because alcohol was affecting my hydration. That abstention was more difficult than you might think. Alcohol is a common coping mechanism in my line of work, and I had just emerged from one of the most stressful experiences in my career.

The second was to coat my feet with surgical spirit for about a week before leaving. This is a liquid that basically hardens the skin. Ballerinas use it to toughen their feet, for obvious reasons. It had always worked for me in the past to prevent blisters and keep the all-important feet robust.

Yeah, I was ready. I thought.

Seven days before we were to set off, the team I'd be climbing with came together for the first time, on a Tuesday night at a local Nairobi restaurant. I knew only one of them, Jake, somewhat well. The second guy I'd met briefly twice and the third was a stranger to me, someone Jake had met at a party. All the way to the meeting, I wrestled with questions. Were we going to get along? Could we trust each other up a mountain? How miserable would it be if one turned out to be a complete idiot? What if I was alienated?

Fortunately, those doubts were short-lived. Before the evening was over it was clear we'd get on very well. We shared backgrounds, kit advice, preparation plans – and I developed my first impressions.

Michiel, a Dutchman in his late forties, was a real explorer, having been in Africa for some time. At the time of our get-together, he'd just returned from Antarctica where he'd spent three weeks with his mum for her eightieth birthday. Clearly he had good genes. It didn't hurt that he was about six-feet-four-inches tall, and strong. His personality made him easy to be around. He was the kind of guy who always had a story or an experience to talk about – and you actually wanted to listen to him. It was done in a modest way, because he was clearly not trying to show off.

Jake, the British guy with whom I'd hiked Mount Kenya, was only an inch shorter than Michiel and fit as a mountain goat. He'd ticked off marathons, ultra-marathons and various rock-climbing adventures. Like Michiel, he knew his stuff. Jake's outstanding characteristic was his very dry sense of humour. With typical British sarcasm, he was able to spot a double entendre in any sentence.

George, a Romanian by birth, was shorter than the other two but powerfully built. He wore his brown hair in a ponytail. He'd left it late in the day to ask what season sleeping bag he needed and whether he would need gloves. Suddenly I felt strong in my kit and ability. That was going to be short-lived. The quietest in the group, George was thoughtful, almost placid. There was nothing offensive about him at all, and beneath that reserve was an obvious compassion for people.

I was the slightest in build of the four of us. Though I stand at six-feet-one and am strong and muscular, I tend to be slim. Okay, wiry. Still, amid the three of them I felt solid, like they'd have my back, and I could have theirs as well.

It was obvious from that first meeting that there was no competition among us. We were interested in each other, what each other had done. They wanted to know about the 14 Riverside attack, which was something that helped break down the conversation barriers, if any existed. It was that interest in each other that immediately began to pull us together.

The one thing I did that the others did not was pack a large notebook – an exercise book like the kind you used in school. I'd started journaling in April of 2018, and although I'd never taken a book and pen with me on any trip, I felt I needed it on this one. Not only did I want to capture my thoughts, feelings and the moments so I could later read about my exploits – I'd also discovered that writing at night rid my mind of the day's events. I had found that I always slept well having written in the journal.

I may not have been ready in the physical ways I should have been, but I was *completely* ready to escape the past month's chaos and seek freedom on the climb. Nairobi was getting back to normal, back to business.

But I was ready to feel the wind in my face and enjoy the spectacular views, my beloved outdoors and all East Africa has to offer. There was some trepidation, naturally, but that was what it was about: living on the edge of my comfort zone.

I just didn't realize how close to teetering on that edge I would come.

CHAPTER SIX

WILL WE EVEN GET THERE?

IN THE WORLD OF BUSINESS there is a strategy known as the *uncertainty advantage.* This is an approach that compels managers to perceive the unknown – such as a recession – as an opportunity to unleash innovative solutions that appeal to customers, investors and so on. It's a chance to go well beyond mere risk management and create new value out of confusion. It was the strategy used by the Hyundai Motor Company in the 2008 global recession, in which they told customers if they bought a car from them and lost their jobs, the company would buy it back with no negative effects on their credit score. It was quite successful.

Getting a transit visa for Uganda put me at a high-uncertainty advantage. I feared the worst and prepared in case. I was going to have to be creative.

A little background: in my usual Crikey, I need to get on this fashion, I waited until late in the preparation process to apply for my visa. Being no stranger to that kind of paperwork, I assumed it would be the proverbial piece of cake and paid my $50 and applied online. Somehow, the fact I hadn't heard anything a day before I was to leave escaped me until that day, so there I was searching the internet for a company that could get me a visa in twenty-four hours. And to no avail.

I wasn't keen on applying through websites that could have been scams, so Plan B was to take myself off to the Ugandan High Commission in the central business district of Nairobi. I had called and been assured they could provide one.

Everything dangerous you can think of goes down in that part of town. In addition to the typical city hustle and bustle, you have robberies and snatches by people on piki piki (Swahili for motorbikes). That got so bad, in fact, that the government banned all such vehicles from the district. And that was just one aspect of the violent crime that took place in the district, especially around the night-time economy. But even in daylight, as a white guy, I was likely to stand out a little.

That was the least of my worries.

There were several awkward conversations with security staff on the gate and at the main door, as well as with a lady in a wooden booth. All were punctuated with eyebrow raising and some tipping of the head to indicate the next route I needed to take, without actually saying anything. What was eventually said was, Nope. The embassy doesn't issue visas – but here's a phone number.

Not quite the result I was looking for. I suspected that number was going to be the start of a wild goose chase. I felt a bit like I was out in a club and, after finding the courage to talk to a pretty girl, I got her number – only to find out it was wrong. Ask me how I know this.

Fortunately, it was not wrong, and that evening I received my visa via email. Everything on it was correct ... except the dates. I'd indicated seven days, which was the length of the climb, but I would actually be in Uganda for ten. By then I had exhausted my skills, and there was nothing for it but to get back on the phone to Immigration Lady #1. She said, "Oh, it will be fine. Just ask them for an extension at the immigration desk on arrival."

I had travelled enough to know that what she said was just not going to happen. At all. An extension requires getting into the country and then heading to the immigration office in a business district to wait for hours for possibly no solution. There was no room in my travel plans for spending a day doing that.

One option remained, and this brings us to what I hoped was my uncertainty advantage. I had my seven-day visa so I could get in. It was getting out that as going to be the issue. What I had in mind was something I'd never tried at a departing airport immigration desk. I was playing some pretty risky odds.

I arrived at Jomo Kenyatta International Airport, checked my bag and headed for the immigration desk, hoping my gamble was going to pay off. In my wallet I had an East African Residency card, which should have allowed me to get an East African free state pass ... 'should' being the operative word.

As I approached, a rather stern-looking man was sitting in his booth behind a protective screen. His entire body was blocked by a computer and his raised desk. This should give you some sense of the guardedness I was about to deal with. It wasn't lost on me either. He was very clearly in charge, and I was going to have to rely on charm to wangle a pass out of him. First step: speak Swahili. Mine is not fluent, but it's at least passably conversational.

Face impassive, he asked where I was going and said, basically, "Give me your boarding pass." Manners are, shall we say, different in Swahili, so there was no "please" or "thank you" involved in this conversation. It's a very direct language. Leta kahawa is "bring coffee". I'd learned that the abruptness is a regional trait and to roll with it. Especially in this circumstance.

As he was thumbing through my heavily stamped passport, I thought, Right now is the time to deploy. So I told him – not abruptly – that I was a resident and needed an East African pass. He looked up, gave me my passport back and said, "Show me."

"With pleasure!" I said, charm fully operational.

I found the page with my handwritten residency recorded. Without saying a word or moving his head, he reached left for a small card.

He wrote something on it, stamped it and handed it to me with my boarding pass. It was indeed an East African pass allowing me free travel across three countries. I thanked him profusely and wished him a good day – siku njema. Anyone watching was probably amused by the sight of a grown man skipping up the stairs to security. Phew! One hurdle down. Now on to the next one.

I met Jake, George and Michiel in the airport cafe to wait for our flight to Entebbe, and it struck me that we were pretty much a disaster in another area of preparation – aside from my visa debacle – and that was our lack of mountain experience as a group. We'd met that once over dinner and then for drinks a week ago. We did get on well, but we had built none of the bonding, rapport and knowledge of personalities required for situations in which we would have to rely on each other when roped together. Aside from that, I'm a person who likes to understand people – what annoys them, what encourages them. I didn't know what would happen if George got hungry or Michiel was tired. That makes a huge difference in how people get on as a group. I was going to have to figure that out while climbing the equivalent of seventeen Eiffel Towers. That might not have given someone else pause, but it did me.

And then there was the next hurdle: the matter of insurance in the event that something went awry. I almost didn't bother with it and only took care of the final details in the taxi on the way to the airport and confirmed it there in the cafe. As it turned out, I didn't estimate the height correctly and was uninsured for the last 400 metres. There were some rolling eyes from the others, but it was all very casual.

I don't want my relaxed attitude to come across as arrogant by any means. I've come to learn there is a wide range when it comes to preparations; everything from the full-out planners who have every detail mapped out and accounted for to those who basically think it'll all work itself out. I was in the middle, and at that point I'll admit I was regretting it.

The flight to Entebbe was short, and as we landed on that hot, humid evening, a full moon beamed down on the airport. I wondered if we could be in store for some of that same beauty on a clear night at the top of the mountain. I'd witnessed a blue blood moon lighting up the skies over Mount Kenya the year before, and my mind began to tingle with the possibilities ahead. We were really doing this.

Our journey from airport to hotel for the night was seamless. I was accustomed to dark, rough roads and the traditional metal-gated compound with security everywhere, and inside the hotel the staff were jovial and happy to offer us food and drinks. Happy to offer, but not as able to comply. Every time one of us said, "May I have the _____?" from the massive menu, the server said, "No." "What about the _____?" "No." This continued for a short while, amid laughter and hysterics on both sides of the counter. Finally, I asked what we could have and, very graciously, we were told water, Nile beer and a Rolex. Not the high-end watch, but a freshly made chapati containing a fried egg. (If you haven't had one, it's well worth giving it a go.) We all ordered that as if we had an actual choice. As for George, he just wanted a beer.

That meant the chef had to be awakened, and, as we waited indoors around a table, we saw him carrying a 25 kg bag of flour into the kitchen. Either he had been well and truly packed up for the night and had to unpack his supplies, or we were going to have a massive chapati.

Nothing like having to trust a grumpy, half-awake chef to prepare your meal. The bonding I was concerned about earlier? It was happening in the midst of that situation, with Jake and I leading the sarcasm.

In the course of the evening – which included a photo shoot of the four of us at the table – I asked the serving ladies where they got the inspiration for the name, Airport Hotel. British sarcasm rarely leaves me, but they were clearly unfamiliar with it, because they launched into a complex explanation of its being only five minutes from the airport. Ya think? Yes, more bonding. Jake was at his best at this point on the sarcasm scale. He was a little bit hangry. But we waited outside and watched a glorious moon, and when the food was ready we found they'd laid the table for a feast, complete with decorative dishes for the chilli sauce.

With a Rolex and a great deal of water downed, I was ready for a decent night's sleep before the next day's true entry into the adventure before us. Didn't happen.

First of all, I felt a little dazed as I stretched out. We each had a private room furnished with a huge bed and the necessary mosquito netting, so I should have been comfortable. Maybe it was the travel – although I travel a good deal. Maybe the oxygen level? Nairobi is at 1,600 metres above sea level, and I was 600 metres lower in Entebbe. I drifted off thinking maybe I was drunk on additional oxygen.

That was the first of many times I fell into sleep those next few hours. It was a hot, sweaty night in which one minute I was kicking off the cover and the next searching for it because I was inexplicably cold. I gave up when it was still dark, took a shower and headed out to eat the breakfast that had been delivered – tea, banana and some biscuits.

One of the hotel staff was walking around the dark garden, and he was quick to tell us that we were late and the bus which was to take us to the airport had already left. Needless to say, this caused a mild panic as we checked our watches and bemoaned the fact there wouldn't be another flight out that day. Was there a time difference we'd forgotten about? Had all of us overslept? There was much googling and confusion, and only George seemed unfazed by it.

And then the gate to the compound opened and the minibus lumbered in. Why the staff guy informed us we'd missed it is still a mystery. Crisis was abated, and the adrenalin rush had shocked us all awake. We loaded our kit into the back of the rickety old vehicle. That minibus was as rough as they come. Everything was falling off it, and George got oil all over him as he climbed in. We were off to an auspicious start.

At any point that morning, I could have turned back. It isn't just that hindsight is 20/20. I saw the signs it wasn't going to be a glamour gig in any way. I told myself that was the fun of it. That was where the adventure came in. Jake was of the same mind, though Michiel was openly questioning what the hell he was doing there. I was just giggling away, thinking this was hilarious.

I boarded the twelve-seat plane – the kind where you can see the cockpit the way you can see the dashboard of a car – right along with my companions. With the pilot and all his dials and buttons and levers clearly in view, we taxied to the end of the runway with the rotor blade spinning. We were lined up as the power rose, and the aircraft began to shake. The louder the engine noise, the harder the vibration. We lurched forward as the plane raced down the runway, and in spite of all indications otherwise, we were airborne.

The wind speed increased from the left side of our tiny plane as it rose into the sky, away from the safety of the runway. If you think of a clock face, the nose was facing toward ten o'clock, but the pilot was trying to fly toward twelve. In essence, we were flying sideways into the skies. To say that it was surreal is not an exaggeration.

Once the plane was righted, along with my stomach, I was able to enjoy the view below. We flew over Lake Victoria and across the villages, rivers and forests of Uganda, which appeared as a quilt of hedgerows, banana trees and dense woods. The roads were like brown veins crisscrossing the countryside amid the grasslands and the deforestation scars and meandering waterways. It was good to get the lie of the land.

The final descent brought us in low over Lake George and a stand of trees with elephants roaming around. The runway at Kasese was grassy, and we taxied straight to a gate in the fence at the edge. One small building on the other side of that fence acted as the departures and arrivals hall. A personal greeting was guaranteed.

Our driver loaded our rucksacks and us into his estate car, which was no easy feat given the size of the four of us and our gear. Bag after bag went into the huge boot, as we each had two. George got in front and the other three of us crammed into the back. To shut the door I had to squeeze over, grab the thing and slam it. If we hadn't bonded before, we would have then. No one could move. We were wedged. We were assured it was a short journey and the roads were fine. I suppose everything is relative.

On our way to the trekking office in the village of Kilembe, the driver told us how heavy rains and melting snow had caused flash floods which brought boulders the size of small cars thundering down the mountain. They knocked through the buildings like bowling balls through skittles. The damage was devastating. Houses that once held mums, dads and children had been destroyed, and a wider river ran where those homes had once stood.

Yet village life continued. There was no choice but to rebuild. I had to admire the resilience of the people in the circumstances they found themselves in. It was a thought that was to come back to me more than once.

We didn't arrive in the village of Kilembe a moment too soon as far as I was concerned. We were crammed into that estate car like commuters on a packed train. You know, breaching every personal space rule but being able to do nothing to avoid it. The car passed through the inevitable gates, where a large number of men sat on a green space as if they were patiently waiting for something. Wearing a mishmash of obviously hand-me-down clothes from a culture not their own, some were lying down, others were propped up on elbows and still others were standing. We learned later that those faces so eager to please were hoping for employment, and a few of them were to become our porters.

The inside of the office was, shall we say, eclectic. Behind the high desk and above the refrigerators, the walls were cluttered with curled and ageing newspaper clippings, one featuring a 78-year-old woman who conquered the mountain. It was oddly reassuring. Even more odd was George's discovery on a bookshelf of a copy of *Fifty Shades of Grey* – translated into Romanian. He gave a little smile and said something about needing that when we came back. It gave new meaning to the word 'random'.

We introduced ourselves at the reception desk and were given the ubiquitous paperwork to complete. Included in that was a thick ledger with its edges curled as if it had been well thumbed over time. It contained the details of anyone and everyone who had ever been into the area.

Because administration is key out there, we all dutifully filled in our names and other requirements. When it came to "Occupation", I was tempted to write "astronaut" – but that wasn't the time for a cheesy line I might have delivered in a club. This was serious; we were going up the Mountains of the Moon.

After filling in the ledger we were handed more paperwork. Initially it looked like your standard disclaimer, but this came with a difference. The last page listed additional costs, including the $10,000-per-hour charge for a helicopter rescue. I knew for a fact that landing a helicopter in that region was far from likely. It would have to come in on an uneven shelf of rock which ... well, it wasn't going to happen. The rescue charge was reduced if you were carried down by guards on a makeshift stretcher, which sounded equally as treacherous. Writing my name on the line beneath the company's refusal to be held responsible for serious injury or death felt like I was literally signing my life away.

With that done, we sat on the old, tatty sofas while the staff rustled up breakfast, which amounted to fruit and some instant coffee. I was hoping for something a little bit more substantial, but the dry humour was the only thing in abundance.

"I have a feeling we did order some pancakes."

"Wide range of choice in this five-star hotel."

Seated in that open area – a roof but no walls – we tucked into it, knowing our bodies needed fuel for the upcoming adventure, and chatted about what we thought we'd be facing. We were still optimistic. The weather was dry. The sun was out. We were looking forward to the views. And we discussed what kit we could leave behind for the way back. We probably wouldn't need those extra socks, right?

We could see the hopefuls by the gate being called into the building to become our porters. Little did we know what they – and we – were about to go through.

CHAPTER SEVEN

WELCOME TO KILEMBE

THE SIGHT OF OUR CHOSEN PORTERS was not reassuring at first. They were obviously strong, as they were about to carry packs that went from their ankles to two or three feet above their heads, at a weight I would hate to guess at. These slim guys were to carry our food, cooking pans and our large rucksacks, while the four of us would have only our day packs on our backs.

But all ten of these very young men were quite small, and each was dressed in ill-fitting clothes, which were second-hand at best, and wellington boots made for sea-level living. Quite frankly, their outfits were something we'd wear out working in our own gardens in the summer. There was definitely nothing professional about these employees, nor would there be. They lived in a once prosperous old tin mining town whose main employment had dried up, and this was the only work available to them.

By contrast, our main guides – Enoch, Roberts and Ochora – were three very strong, smart-looking Ugandan guys in professional uniforms of black trousers and very bright yellow shirts with their names embroidered on them. They worked for the trekking company and were very clearly experienced. They were up and down the mountains many times a year.

Roberts was a short, quiet guy, and very calm. Ochora was his opposite: stern, sharp and always standing bolt upright in military fashion – feet apart, hands behind his back, chest out. Let's just say he had probably seen some other action in these parts. Enoch, however, was the leader. He had a permanent smile. Seriously, he never lost that perpetual grin for the next seven days.

As Enoch introduced the other two and continued with a brief of what we were about to embark on, I found him to be cool, calm and professional. He explained our route using the map on the wall, though from what I could gather, we were simply going up and up along paths and various "zones". The snow and ice, he assured us, would be firm and the chances of rain very slim. He was saying what I wanted to hear: we would summit on a clear day to amazing views. It would be rugged, cold – and simply beautiful. He didn't minimize the challenge, but I was fine with that. I kept my mind on the liberation of reaching the tops of these mountains and seeing how insignificant we are in this powerful, natural world.

Once the briefing was over, we collected our wellington boots, which we were convinced to take, and strapped them onto our bags. Then off we marched to the gates of the compound, past the other porters waiting for business, and made our way up a slight incline through the village.

That was an experience in itself. A tethered cow grazing. Goats roaming around looking for small pieces of grass to gobble up. Chickens chasing each other about. Women washing clothes and laying out fruit to sell.

The most interesting, however, were the kids. They stopped abruptly in their playing to openly stare at this group of four white guys walking up the middle of the road; four men seemingly off to battle passing through their beautiful, bustling village. The young girls in their dresses stood off to the side, while the bolder boys ran up to high-five us, shouting *mzungu*, the Swahili word for white foreigner. Depending on how it's said, the word can be interpreted as incredibly derogatory, so I don't suggest adding it to your vocabulary. As we passed the busy school yard, I realized the squealing-laughing-yelling sounds of playgrounds don't change wherever you are in the world.

We left the small village behind and hiked up a steep, direct but very pot-holed, water-damaged track, which didn't stop a motorbike coming up at a slow speed carrying a passenger. It wove its way ahead of us, trying to miss the massive holes, but the driver got it understandably stuck. As a unit we helped pull him out – lifted the pannier on the back of the bike and extricated it from the rut. No discussion. We just did it, which was heartening. We were turning into a team.

Further on we caught up with a group of teenagers seemingly in good spirits, some carrying plastic chairs upside down on their heads, others holding hands and laughing. Their English wasn't good, our Swahili was only slightly better and our knowledge of their local language was non-existent, but we managed to understand, to our surprise, that they were taking the hike up to the cemetery, as a young man in the village had died. They were in high form for what you'd expect would be a sombre journey, but the language barrier prohibited our learning what that was about.

We parted ways with them at a fork in the path and took a gentle right around a corner and along a narrow trail about two feet wide. Looking down on the right we could see plantations – avocado, banana and coffee – and, not far into the distance, a powerful river with its remnants of displaced rocks from the flash flood. Up the hill on the other side, which mirrored our side, were small, family mud huts where children played on the nearly vertical land. The people were hard workers. It was dusty out there but they always had huge smiles on their faces. No running water, no electricity and certainly no gas, but in one sense they reminded me of my friends and me back in the day: they didn't need a lot to have fun; they just needed to make sure they took full advantage of the daylight.

It was clear to me that living there required hard work, and getting up as the sun rose to make the most of the day. Mums directed the children to fetch water and help on the farm, basically teaching them how to live off the land that provided them with food and also stock to sell. Yet their life was refreshingly simple. The air was fresh and crisp as it is only in the mountains. The water rumbled and raged in the background, promising a full supply. I could feel the stress falling from my shoulders.

This was a nice, gentle way to start the day. We entered the park itself, which was at 1,700 metres, and checked in at the warden's hut – a small brick building with a roof and, of course, the traditional long-drop toilet. Yeah, the loo was a hole in the ground with a questionable roof, walls and a million flies whizzing around. We'd come to expect that as the standard toilet style, but the number of flies was unusual, and it indicated someone might have died in there ...

The porters stopped for a rest and lay out on the wooden benches, or just on the ground. This was when it became really obvious to me the amount of stuff they were carrying in those large polypropylene sacks. They were huge and – this blew me away – instead of handle straps over their shoulders like our rucksacks, they had a thinner piece of fabric stitched into the outer side of the sack which they used to lift it and then put that fabric across their forehead. It was the forehead that took all the weight, meaning their upper backs and neck muscles were immensely strong. My admiration for them was increasing by the minute.

Once we were registered, in yet another dog-eared ledger, we officially entered the park. For such a grand adventure, the entrance was far from impressive. It was nothing more than a gap in aluminium hoardings about the width of the road with a metal fence extending left and right and uphill into the distance. Just inside were the foundations for more buildings, barely hopeful of ever being completed. It felt a bit like we were entering a new world where only the brave went.

Silence descended around us. We were the only ones there, and we were not likely to see anyone else until we came off the mountain in six days' time. Michiel commented that it seemed as if we were leaving one world behind and entering something different. I wasn't as eloquent. I just said it felt like we were entering our own version of Jurassic Park.

We still had a lot of day left. Of course it was hot and humid, as evidenced by the sweat running down my forehead and dripping off my nose, and I noticed my breathing had already changed. I was having to suck in air more deeply, though we could still carry on a conversation, through which I learned that Enoch had been up this mountain over 400 times. So ... 400 times he'd been in and out of the Bamboo Zone we were currently making our way through. Each time I see bamboo now, I can imagine the sweat flooding (no exaggeration) down my face and taste the dust in the air as we pumped upwards on a hill that grew steeper at every step. With the altitude increasing and the oxygen decreasing, I'd soon had enough of the Bamboo Zone.

But none of that was different to what I'd expected. And it was more than worth it when we crossed the river into a spectacular sight: a small waterfall making a thunderous noise, its crisp droplets clearing the air. Standing on the drier rocks, we stopped and took in the view of the water rushing down the mountain and over the edge, crashing on to the large boulders. It struck me that rivers flow in the most efficient way. I love that they stand for no nonsense, and if they come up against a problem, they don't stop. They go around it.

We took a moment to wash in this chilled water, a moment to look down the valley to the river flowing off into the greenery below. But our moments of quiet serenity were shattered by Enoch, who informed us we were about to head up a very sharp incline that would require us to climb, though not with ropes. Typically the ropes are not brought out unless the climb is vertical. As we four, sweat-drenched men embarked on that climb – and can I just say "very sharp" was an understatement – there was no conversation. While we were busting our lungs, the guides were promising the journey was easy. I wasn't going to be the first to disagree.

In fact, when we stopped briefly under a tree, sheltered from the blistering sun, I looked at Jake's soaking wet back when he took off his rucksack and said, "Whose great idea was this again?"

I was joking, of course, and they picked up on the pure sarcasm dripping from my voice and agreed. Especially Jake. Besides, the next gradient was more gentle, and the river flowing to our right and the sunbeams striking through the forest canopy made up for all of it. This was nature at her purest. We stopped at a small, open area and tucked into our lunches sitting on tree stumps and man-made benches. Although calling it lunch was questionable. The sandwiches had been squished in our rucksacks, like they'd been in the bottom of someone's school bags for a week. It felt good to rest, but the sweat started to chill us, and we had to get moving again as quickly as possible.

Whether they said this to all their trekkers I had no idea, but the guides commented on our strong pace as we moved upwards on trails that were merely dusty paths littered with tree roots. As the oxygen level lowered, they told us we were nearly at the first hut. Yes, it was only a few kilometres away, but it was all uphill. I learned that first day that their idea of "nearly there" was far different from ours. Even when Enoch proclaimed, "We are there!", we still had 200 metres – vertical metres – to go.

The camp was made up of wooden huts painted yellow and raised slightly off the ground on concrete pillars to allow flood water to flow underneath. A small stick structure covered in a blue tarpaulin with cracks in it to let smoke escape was the "kitchen", where I discovered the chef crouching over a small fire and stirring a pot of what I assumed to be dinner. The flames were inviting, because now that we'd stopped walking and the day was drawing to a close, the gentle breeze was chilling.

Our hut, with its curved roof, looked like an old caravan wagon without wheels, but the view from its front was resort-worthy. Stretching out before us was a spectacular view of the valley – the jagged mountain peaks, the glaciers, the forest – and our journey so far. Behind us were the rugged snow-caps enveloped in dramatic, swirling clouds.

Our private bath outside the hut consisted of an upturned water carrier seated in a wire stand equipped with a bar of soap. A small wooden square housed our hole-in-the-ground toilet. After a full day of walking uphill, I had to face the long-drop toilet. That is when having done squats came in handy, although my legs felt as if they were being stabbed with knives.

While the other three guys unpacked, I lay on my back with my legs in the air, resting my lower calves on the upper bunk. I'd heard that helps drain any lactic acid that's built up in the muscles. Whatever it did, after ten or fifteen minutes I felt better and was ready for my next slightly bold plan.

It may not seem bold on the face of it. I made a short hobble past the other huts (where the guides and porters were staying in their own community of sorts) along a path to the stream. A good enough area – meaning it was relatively dry, with a tree root where I could put my clothes and some concealing trees so I could strip down. Standing there in my boxers, putting my feet in the water one at a time and letting it rise over my body ... suddenly I was a kid on holiday on the south coast of England heading into the sea.

I hadn't planned on getting totally submerged. The getting in required a small jump into the very clear water, but it was still not wise to ever jump into a pool like that. I also needed to think about how I would get out. Injuring myself would put the mockers on the mountain summit plan. I just wanted to squat and splash off the sweat.

As I leaned forward and scooped the water up, I gasped because it was almost freezing. Quickest wash-up on record, but oh how grateful I was for the fresh water washing over my body. That was followed by the clothing routine. The routine made me feel a million dollars. It called for a day set of clothes and a night set, for a couple of reasons. One, I wouldn't feel totally dirty all the time, and that does get old even when you're anticipating it. And two, the day's sweat doesn't stay in the clothes as the evening chill sets in. Getting out of them and into the night-time clothes is a treat that I'd do well to stick to.

Dinner that night was a mountain of food: potatoes, vegetables and meat with gravy. Our bodies needed to replace lost energy and store up some for the next day, and I ate until I couldn't put another mouthful into my stomach. And then there was the Ugandan coffee to be had before we were off to bed at 8 p.m.

My new sleeping bag lived up to expectations. I shed my thermals and socks and snuggled in to recount the day. It had become my nightly habit to list all I was thankful for, and on that good Day One, the list was long. The flight – and the survival of our sideways take-off. The pilot and his obvious skill. The minibus driver who proved our steward wrong. The impossible porters. The mysterious trio of guides. The chef and the meal he produced with his improbable fire. The clothing – night and day. The gradually bonding team. The hut. The four-season bag. The peaceful sleep I was about to fall into. Before I drifted off, I thought about the river we'd seen earlier, flowing and bouncing and bobbing and weaving but always finding its way through. I realized I was kind of like that. If someone says it can't be done, I'm all about 'maybe not yet, but let's find a way'. Everything is a challenge, so why not have a go? Some people are reservoirs, happily living with their lot in life. As for me, I'm a river.

Whose idea was this? I'd asked. I couldn't remember and it didn't matter. I only knew I was grateful to whoever it was.

CHAPTER EIGHT

THIS IS THE DRY SEASON, RIGHT?

EVERYTHING IS RELATIVE when you're on a mountain trek. Things that would bother you in your day-to-day life are just normal stuff up there and need to be taken in stride. If you can't wrap your mind around that, you'd be better off turning around and heading back to the bottom and maybe having a go at it another time.

That applies to the effects on your body. We did some injury assessment that first night. Michiel had sore red heels, so he simply taped them up. Jake was all good and so was George. I had a slight warming on the underside of my big right toe, but nothing to be concerned about. Basically, that was just the usual wear and tear. Even the bodies of the most fit will react to anything different from the daily physical stressors.

Sleep that night wasn't the best, but I got some rest. The sleeping bag was warm to the point of too-hot, so I had to escape it for a while, though fortunately my dry bag stuffed with clothes made do as a pillow. As for breakfast the next morning, we were treated to cold porridge, but food is fuel no matter how unappetizing.

It was all just business as usual. We First World folks are probably too soft anyway.

We set off straight into the climb at 9 a.m. – straight up. The trail was immediately steep – though not so much so that we needed ropes – and got my heart pumping nearly out of my chest. There were no warm-up sessions on this tour. The route was a muddy path littered with twisting tree roots which, on the one hand kept the soil together but, on the other, will slip you up when wet.

Did I mention wet? Not long after we took off up the mountain that day, the rain came. Not a sprinkle or a shower – it was a full-on torrent that lasted for three solid hours as we walked up streambeds looking for boulders or solid patches of greenery to stand on.

It was supposed to be the dry season.

Still, stiff upper lip and all that. The looks on my fellow climbers' faces were blank, but I could see the despair. Especially in Michiel. His jacket and rucksack weren't waterproof enough, and he donned a hooded white plastic poncho over everything. He looked like nothing less than a giant Casper the Ghost. Perhaps minus the Friendly.

It couldn't possibly go on much longer. Even when the seams on the inside of my trusty Gore-Tex jacket gave out, I chalked that up to the fact that I'd been wearing it since 1991. It had had a good go. Of course, that meant my fleece got soaked and then my T-shirt. Since that was tucked into my trousers, my boxer shorts were the next victims of the drenching. Being wet is not pleasant. All right, it's miserable, but there wasn't a lot I could do except keep going. I had a back-up jacket. The end was in sight.

Yet I'll admit I was feeling a little bit rubbish. And I wasn't the only one. Something wasn't quite right with our George. He was having to take off his shoes and wring out his socks, and the extra ones we'd left at the camp came to mind. George was not one to share his emotions, so he didn't say much. But I learned later his feet were soaked, which put him in danger of getting a modern-day version of trench foot. Not surprising, given the amount of water and mud that was seeping in.

Our stop – which couldn't have come soon enough in my view – was at a collection of derelict huts. My first move was to get out of my wet clothes; not an easy task, as the T-shirt wanted to cling to my body. It reminded me of being a kid learning to swim. One of the tests was to wear pyjamas while treading water for forty-five minutes and then take them off, tie a knot in the end and blow them up to act as a float. I can't remember whether I passed. All I recall was that they stuck to me like glue as I wrestled to remove them. Just like now. Add to this that, as you get the wet clothes off, your skin is wet, and the chilly, windy air soon whips in and gives you an extra little chill, encouraging you to get some other clothes on ASAP.

Once in a dry shirt, a fresh fleece and my back-up waterproof jacket, we were off again. I was still wearing wet boxers but there was nothing for that at that moment.

Again, everything is relative. As we left the dilapidated camp, I dropped my 1991 Gore-Tex into the bin and bade it farewell. I wasn't convinced the substitute was going to sustain the elements for long if the rain persisted, but there was no way the forlorn Gore-Tex would.

This was the dry season.

Short parts of the trail had a boardwalk – a path made of pretty decent planks of wood and supporting posts and joists. They were occasionally sturdy, sometimes wobbly and always short-lived, but a very welcome respite from the wet underfoot. In a word: fantastic. Even as I was enjoying the respite from rocky climbing, I imagined the effort people must have gone to carrying all that lumber up to these heights, just to make a decent pathway across the swamplands for us and other like-minded explorers. I really was grateful for what we had, and it was a joy to feel like we were upping the pace and gaining ground quickly towards the next stop.

It became increasingly difficult as the rain continued to pelt us. At that altitude we realized how quickly the cold can set in, and when you pause from strenuous activity the chill takes hold abruptly, so our lunch stop by a rocky outcrop was brief. There were no blankets, hampers and Tupperware containers. This was grab the squashed food from the side pocket of the rucksack, eat quickly and get up and get on. Everyone was shivering and moving about, which was not an easy task in the howling wind. This was no longer 'just-the-way-it-is-on-a-mountain trek'.

We finally made it to the Bugata camp for the night. At 4,062 metres, it appeared to also serve as a helicopter landing pad. Just in case. The camp itself consisted of four plastic tents constructed to look like a wagon without wheels. There were two sets of bunk beds inside, and the wind whipped in, with the plastic only taking off the worst edge. The whole set-up was on a rocky surface overlooking … well, not a lot. The clouds obstructed any view we might have had.

I wasn't up for taking in a vista anyway. All any of us wanted to do was get out of our second set of wet clothes for the day and into dry ones. Except that our main bag contents arrived soaked through. We are talking past the rucksack's protective shell, through the rucksack itself and into the dry bags. We were less than impressed. To say it had rained relentlessly is an absolute understatement.

And yet our spirits weren't dampening, so there was that. We kept assuring each other the downpour would stop and we could enjoy the rest of the climb. Any crankiness we felt was the result of being tired and hungry, and even then we relied on our basic sarcasm to pull us through.

Enoch, of course, was still smiling.

Actually, there was no time for moaning. We were in a wet environment in a damp tent with no real heating, but we had to get out of the drenched clothes and put on dry ones. And clean off the day's sweat, which had still managed to ooze, even in the chill.

There was some water for washing hands and face in an upturned carrier in a wire stand. It was actually too cold to do anything but look at it; water on the face was like landing face-first in the snow. Wet Wipes were the only thing that could make me feel human and slightly fresh. No matter that I'd have to get into the same sweaty clothes the next day. For now I had to focus on the moment. Get these clothes off, get the night ones on and do it quickly. The air was gasp-worthy.

The end tent, joined to ours by a small boardwalk, had a small area for "dining". That consisted of a table and two benches, but more importantly it possessed a small log-burner. A small collection of wet wood was scooped up by us and the porters. At that altitude, wood burns a great deal more slowly than at sea level – particularly when it's wet – but we were all keen to try to dry our socks and T-shirts.

It took all evening.

And when we were done, everything we owned smelled of woodsmoke. The stuff that made it, anyway. One of my shirts got too close to the flame and ended with some extra ventilation holes with hard, burnt fabric edges, but it was a layer of clothing. I started to realize how important each piece was.

In the kitchen hut, which was big enough to hold five or six and a couple of small cooking pots, fires burned, food was being boiled and men were cleaning pots and pans, all while steam and smoke billowed out the door. The result – rather ingeniously and a long time later – was an enormous meal which we could only devour part of. That meant copious leftovers for the porters, whom I was appreciating more by the hour.

It's always the case that with good food in your stomach you can be a lot more optimistic, and you can sleep well and give your body the energy it needs to replenish, recover and reset for the next day. The mist was clearing. Our kit was getting less wet – though it's a bit too much to say it was drying – and we left for our hobbit tent in the hope what we'd put on tomorrow wouldn't be half bad. The rain would stop. We would salvage the trip, and we would see this rugged mountain range clearly and in all its glory.

Even though I could see my breath as I lay in the bottom bunk wrapped up and zipped up, I wrote in my notebook, head torch on, capturing the moments of the day. At that point, despite the disappointments, I was still basically just recounting what happened, exercising my mind. There were no profound conclusions to come to. Yet.

I was thinking about the top, though. In my mind was the peak as I'd watched it on those YouTube videos where the summit was beautiful and the views amazing. I pictured clear, crisp glaciers – experienced in my imagination the freedom of being up there. Of being at that high place.

Little did I know how low I was to be taken.

When I awoke at 7 a.m. I was the first up, so crept into my daytime clothes and outside to peer over the edge of the precipice we were camped on. But I could still see nothing. Absolutely nothing. Dense mists had descended, obliterating both where we'd been and where we were going. That was okay. At least it wasn't raining.

Until 9 a.m. when we were packed up and ready to continue our ascent. Then the torrent came down just as it had the day before, and we headed straight into it. My fingers were securely crossed in the hope that my substitute jacket would hold out.

Naturally the first bit was a heart-pumping uphill section. The gloves were on and already getting a good soaking. But we'd done it yesterday. We could do it again today. As we got higher, however, the rain became sleet. And then hail. Bizarrely, the hail was a pleasant sight. It just bounced off our jackets instead of seeping straight through to the skin.

As we moved on through it, I was checking in on everybody to see if they were okay. I always seem take on that role on hikes and climbs. The French word for it in cycling is 'domestique'. I'm always moving front, then back, flexibly, to make sure all is well with everyone. The responses that day were:

"Loving the rain."

"This is great."

"Views are amazing."

Even George and Michiel were getting the hang of sarcasm.

We finally reached 4,500 metres. Only to begin an immediate descent that looked and felt like a ninety-degree incline – which of course it wasn't. But by then it seemed no matter where we turned, there was something else coming at us. Rain. Sleet. Hail. A downhill climb that meant before long there would be an uphill one just as challenging. And this downhill wasn't just a walk downhill. This was jumps, steps, down makeshift ladders competing with the newly made rivers flanked either side by the plants, shrubs and trees.

The steps, even for someone who is six-feet-one, were big, and planting my foot down meant a shudder going up through the knee into the body. As I took the next step down, I attempted to soften the landing by either sitting to get down, or holding on to a tree, a branch, anything just to break up the nearly out-of-control body dropping like a stone.

Onward we went in the pouring rain until we reached a muddy swamp. There was no going round that. There were limited tree roots to give us sanctuary from going waist-deep in seconds. I had experienced this in 1993 in Dartmoor – a huge expanse in the west country of England, made up of vast, open moorlands and valleys. A prison was built there so if someone escaped they would have no clue which way to go. As police cadets, when we were faced with those swamps, we found ourselves either jumping or taking giant steps to tufts of grass or dead animals to give us a moment to quickly think where our next step would come to save us from falling in. It didn't work in Dartmoor.

And it wasn't working there on a steep downhill slope. I had to wonder: had it really been a path at any point? Had anyone ever gone that way before? Were we the first to be routing through there? To a man we were all saying some version of Holy Fuck! We were literally walking down a fast-moving, muddy river. If lava could have been wet mud, that's what it was like – soaking us up and taking us with it. Each step sank us up to knee, desperate to get that foot out before it sucked us in. Left or right, it didn't matter. I felt as if I was playing jungle manoeuvres, only it was cold. And downhill.

We were approaching lunch time, and I could feel myself becoming fatigued and nearly at the point of sense of humour failure. It takes a lot to get me to that place, and it qualified as a lot. The whole thing was becoming torturous, and I kept muttering to myself, "Really? A break, please?" I was cold, I was wet and I just needed to sort my kit out and get some food on board.

Lunch didn't provide much of one. We stopped on a cold, rocky outcrop with just a piece of metal to act as shelter. I was wet and freezing and, just as I'd feared, the back-up jacket was failing. I was not as bad off as George, though, who was visibly shivering. Although his feet must have been saturated, he didn't take his shoes off this time.

We all shivered through some food and began another climb – one that suddenly descended again into a treacherous path. Make no mistake: a downhill trudge is as difficult as going up. This one was steep and boggy up to the knees, as we were basically fording a river formed by the rain charging down the mountain. We ploughed through dense undergrowth and rocks we couldn't see. It struck me at one point that there was no animal activity about. They clearly had more sense than we did.

Enoch continued to be cheerful. "Just over this ridge!" he called out to us. The rain was biblical, yet he kept motivating us just a little further – four times, which made it hard to trust him after the second assurance.

I supposed he was using some kind of psychology. I'd probably tried that on my kids when they were young to keep them quiet in the back seat of the car, but truly, it's a flawed motivational strategy. "Just over this ridge!" worked once, but after a few times I started to question the legitimacy of the statements. I was practically despairing by the time "just over this ridge" did bring us to our stopping place.

The hail had reverted to torrential rain, and we were delighted to see that a fire had been started and there were lights in the hut. This time the hut was bigger, and the centrepiece was a wood-burning stove which porters were stocking up with wet wood, hoping it would burn. There was indeed a great deal of hoping going on.

Spirits lifted somewhat. Jake and I were laughing again. George went off for some much needed alone time. Enoch told us, smiling of course, how he'd built all the huts. The structure was somewhat unusual, but we couldn't be too harsh. They were still standing. The race was on to hang wet socks, T-shirts – and even someone's sleeping bag that had succumbed to the elements – from every hook and rafter we could find until the place looked like a laundry. While the rain poured, the wind battered the shed, whipping open one of the doors and belting us with cold air. We never did get that door to completely close again; it was like it was haunted by some kind of poltergeist.

At least steam was rising from the damp clothing, which had to mean dryness was forthcoming. It also meant some of our kit got burned, including another one of my T-shirts and my down jacket in a few places. I was able to get my socks dry. When you don't have masses, you tend to treasure what you have, and I had sticking plasters. The down jacket was repaired.

As a group we focused on the stove, where we hovered to get some warmth back into our bones. Once our laundry was hung, we discussed our near sense of humour failure. It was perhaps the chocolate that someone produced and shared that got us to the place where we could laugh when we said to each other, "What are we doing here?"

We had our usual evening briefing with the ever-grinning Enoch. The whole team was enthusiastic, so clearly they knew something we didn't. I'll admit to being relieved when Enoch said tomorrow would be an easy three-hour hike, which would give us time at the end of the day to get our kit sorted, get some sleep and be ready for the 2 a.m. rise to make the peak.

Just two and a half days until we reached the pinnacle I'd been dreaming about? We could do that. I could do that. Frozen, rugged landscape? No problem. Above me were crisp, clear skies and an abundance of stars, and as I wrote in my notebook that night, I allowed some of the bonkers things I come up with to spill out onto the page. Do you get to see more stars from this, the fattest part of the planet? So close to the equator, wouldn't that make sense?

It was a good sign that I was thinking playfully again. The human spirit can be indomitable if we allow it to be.

However, there are the circumstances that threaten to take our spirit down and stomp on it. I was about to discover what those looked like.

CHAPTER NINE

YOU ARE NOT GOING TO DIE ON ME

THE NEXT MORNING, the demoralizing rain continued. It poured and poured as if buckets were being emptied above us, and I couldn't imagine going out into that wet, frozen landscape again. Enoch's imagination was apparently more vivid than mine because he was ready to lead us onward, smiling as always. I was beginning to wonder if he slept with that grin on his face.

I myself was not in a jovial mood, and I raised the point that since we only had a three-hour hike ahead of us, we could hold off an hour to see if the rain would subside. I got no push-back. Everyone was wet and aching and in agreement.

We all waited inside that windy wooden shed, the doors flying open with each strong gust of wind. But we were out of the weather, where we could just let the time pass. We hung out with our tea and the fire and tried to enjoy a little respite – 'tried' being the operative word.

An hour brought no relief. Though we had rested a little longer, the rain continued to whip up. There was nothing for it; we had to go out.

Enoch's solution was to advise us to wear our wellington boots instead of our hiking boots (which we would save for the summit attempt) because we were going to go through some very swampy land, and the wellies with their rubber soles would provide a good grip on the rocks.

That wasn't "very swampy land" we'd sloshed through the day before?

We donned said boots and set out through what was more a cold riverbed than a swamp. It didn't take long to become hot on the inside, cold on the outside, probably because the waterproof jacket wasn't doing its job. Actually, in those conditions, I would have been surprised if any jacket could have dealt with the inner and outer battering it was getting.

The temperature changed, but not for the better. As it dropped, the wind increased, and the rain turned to hail which slashed at my face. All of this was an attitude challenge as well as a physical one. The choice was constantly going through my mind: should I stop, turn around or keep going? At least we could still smile through the question we were all voicing: Now THIS? Really? We had all taken a sucker punch at that point, even the porters. We were literally being battered by the elements, and it was getting to be a little too much. The mantra I muttered quietly to myself as I plodded forward became Give us a break. Give us a BREAK!

Part of the day's trek included clambering from boulder to boulder, like we may all have done as kids, pretending the floor was hot lava or crocodile-infested waters and the furniture was the only safe haven. This was a real-life game, however, which would have been enjoyable in dry weather, but not so much in what was snow. We couldn't see the rocks we were supposedly jumping to. The boulders of varying sizes and shapes weren't going to give us a flat platform to jump onto, with each one providing its own twist or edge to test our patience.

By the third hour we were in the middle of a snowstorm, which answered the question, "It can't get much worse, can it?" We carried on uphill, one step at a time. I think. I couldn't actually feel my freezing feet. Wellington boots with several pairs of thick socks couldn't hold out the cold. I was only aware that they were like frigid stones inside my boots. My face was faring little better. It felt as if it had been sandblasted by everything weather could dish out: rain, hail, sleet – and now snow.

There was a small wooden structure ahead which we focused on, hoping to get a little respite from the brutal conditions. It was difficult to make out exactly what the structure was through the greyness of the clouds and the whiteness of the snow. We continued, and as we got closer I realized it wasn't going to provide any shelter. At all. It was just a roof. Wind and snow swirled around in what inside there was. We didn't stop for long. Stopping meant getting cold, and getting cold was to be avoided.

There wasn't much speaking going on. Each of us was in our own world, focusing. I still wanted to keep an eye on where the team was and stopping should one fall back, but Jake and George had continued on, so we were strung out more than before. Even the porters and the guides were struggling upward. Their pace was slower than usual, but they kept on, hard as nails yet clearly suffering.

They wore ill-fitting clothes, not one item of which appeared waterproof. Some had ratty shirts and jackets that weren't fit for much of anything. In their sacks made of raffia, a natural woven fibre, they were carrying not only our kit but a small amount of firewood, and they asked us to collect some as we ascended because there would be none for fires to warm us up nor dry our clothes where we were headed. I had no idea how they weren't literally freezing, but they continued on.

After what was, in reality, longer than three hours, we reached Margherita Camp, from which we would attempt the summit at 3 a.m. the next morning. The first wooden shed at the camp was a welcome sight to all of us. Both my big toes felt as if they were no longer there, and my outer clothes were wet down to the fleece layer. Below the fleece was a thermal layer which seemed to be holding in nothing but sweat. It wasn't a pleasant feeling, and although I didn't get a glimpse in a mirror, I was certain it wasn't a good look either. We were a motley crew – although really, who cared? All we wanted to do was get out of those wet, sweaty clothes and into dry ones.

Inside the first shed was a wood-burner, but no fire yet because the only wood available was what we brought. The terrain was virtually nothing but rocks in a snowy atmosphere, dotted with a few huts for sleeping and two long-drop toilets. We abandoned our kit quickly in our sleeping hut and headed back to the main one to see if we could get some warmth going.

Just three small wooden steps led up to the hut, but even those provided a challenge to our wilting bodies. The building was little more than an oversized yellow shed with a wooden door that seemed to blow open on its own when not held partially shut by a lump of rock, although the icy wind blew right through the opening even when it was sort of closed.

Inside, the hut was sparse, featuring a blackened wood-burner in the middle with the familiar rails on the side, perfect for hanging wet items to dry. If only the thing was lit. We had a go with what we had: damp kindling, wet wood and some matches. It started but quickly went out, and all we could do was persevere. And can I just say that perseverance does not keep you warm? We each had a go at it, and it just wasn't working. Our only bit of joy at that point was warmth, and we weren't getting it. Any kind of mirth had disappeared. In fact, it would have been easy to take a chunk out of someone, just out of sheer irritation, but that wouldn't have helped, so we stayed quiet.

To the right were a table and a few chairs, and to the right of those another small table with some cups on it, but no sign of any hot drinks yet. At the far end was what looked like a staff section, separated by a standard bench for sitting and a few bowls that would hopefully become containers for the washing-up and the cooking water. Although that expectation was getting thinner by the minute.

Our one real hope was the small Jiko – a clay pot with a grill on its top – where the chef was trying to warm the wet wood the porters had supplied, just to dry it out so we could create a fire. It looked as if some of the team were off to get more from the sacks, while the rest were gathered, chatting.

They were seemingly oblivious to the young porter leaning against the shed wall – who didn't look so great.

He was a short Ugandan man wearing a ripped cotton '80s ski jacket that appeared to have no insulation – the kind you may have worn on a warm autumnal day to walk down to the pub. He wore no gloves or hat, and he was soaking wet. It was no wonder he was visibly trembling.

He was standing slightly bent forward at the waist, his arms somehow frozen in front of him, but at the same time violently shaking. Imagine them bent at the elbow and his hands turned in as if each was holding a glass in crippled fingers. I could see him changing colour – his skin going from warm brown to almost-grey, his lips turning blue – and his eyes were sinking into vacancy in his head. It looked to me like he was suffering from hypothermia in its advanced stage. A quick judgement call captured all that was happening, and the thought: this guy is not long for this world.

I went over to him, calling George along the way. The porter looked even worse close up. There was almost no life in his eyes, and he was nearly unresponsive.

But I talked to him anyway: "Listen. Listen to me. We're going to warm you up."

I doubt he understood me. My London accent can cause words to get lost for the basically non-English speaker. In the situation, I was sure he wasn't focusing on what I was saying anyway, but I've found that clear commands can get a situation under control, even if the words themselves aren't understood.

Then I turned and yelled out, "Does anyone have any dry clothing at all?"

Somebody produced a fleece, while George and I peeled off the poor man's wet clothes and let them fall to the floor. I was virtually shouting to him, telling him what we were doing. He looked deep into my eyes, faintly pleading for help, just before his own eyes rolled completely back into his head.

"Don't you die," I shouted to him. All the death I'd seen recently was like a force, driving me. I could do with not seeing someone lose his life in front of me again. So I continued to shout, "You are not going to die on me. Don't you f--ing dare."

Once we had him zipped up in the fleece, I said to George, "Stand in front of him and hold him real tight like you're cuddling him."

I got behind the young porter, sandwiching him in as I stretched my arms around him and held on to George. I've got to say I wasn't the warmest of people but, by comparison, I was an oven. Still, just standing there holding him wasn't going to increase his body temperature. He remained rigid.

111

"We've got to get him moving," I said to George.

He looked at me from his bearded face like I'd just grown an additional head. WHAT? We'd just hiked all day, uphill, in rain, snow and hunger. And I wanted him to move some more?

I wasn't in the best shape either, but I said, adamantly, "George! We've got to warm this guy up."

He nodded. Holding on to George's clothes, I pulled the porter in even tighter and kept repeating some semblance of, "You'll be great. You'll be warm. You'll be fine." To be honest, I didn't have a clue whether he would be or not.

"We're going to run on the spot," I said to George.

He shook his head. "I'm too exhausted."

"It won't take long," I said.

Actually, that was a lie, but it worked. George joined me as we ran on the spot with this guy between us. You only have to picture that for a second to realize how awkward it was, but all I could think of was to generate heat. I felt no pain, no fatigue. I could only focus on warming up his core.

At that altitude, within minutes both George and I were puffing and panting and sweating with the exertion, though even that didn't really register in my mind.

But George wasn't quite there, and I couldn't blame him. We'd had an impossible three days and we hadn't even begun to thaw.

"I can't do this," he told me. "I'm wiped out."

"We have to keep going," I said. "If we don't, this little guy is going to die."

I called over my shoulder for the others to get that fire started and get me some hot water. The porter needed hot, sugary tea, and he needed it fast.

"I have to stop." I looked at George, who at this point wasn't faring much better than our hypothermic porter. "I'm running out of oxygen."

"Just a little longer," I said. And somehow I kept us going.

I have told this story a few times both in formal and informal settings. After one recent presentation, a woman from the audience approached me and said, abruptly, "Why?"

My obvious response was, "Why what?"

"Why did you try to save him? Obviously no one else cared."

I didn't give her the answer that whipped immediately into my mind, which was, "Are you serious?" I even double-checked to make sure I'd understood her right. I had. How was I supposed to respond to that?

What I did tell her was that the young porter was a human being and I highly value human life, no matter whose it is. Besides, he was in essence suffering because he was doing something for me, for all of us.

But there was more to it than that, really. For years I have spent time running towards danger or keeping an eye out for potentially treacherous situations, always scanning and looking and soaking up. It's something of a curse, and at times I wish I could be more oblivious, because when I see a threat, I will do my level best to avoid, thwart or help whoever is teetering on the edge of disaster. I'm not a superhero. When it comes to flight or fight, I just naturally tend to fight to the best of my ability.

And on this occasion our guy needed my level best. It wasn't about the fact that he was paid a small amount of money per day and was considered by some to be less important than any of us. It was about the fact that he was a human and had a mum and dad, maybe siblings, maybe even a wife and kids of his own. No matter the person, no matter his situation, being kind and considerate has to be the front runner. Those were the same thoughts I'd had at the mortuary back in Nairobi, and it was all too sharp an image. I was going to do all I could to keep him alive.

I've no idea where the saying 'level best' originates from but, for me, it was based on one question: was there anything I wouldn't do to make the situation right? I can think of nothing more we could have tried in order to save his life. If stripping out of my own clothes would have helped, I would have done it, but that would only have made me a candidate for hypothermia, and we both would have ended up dead. But I become quite stressed when I can't reach that best in a difficult situation.

Where that comes from, I don't know. It simply kicks in. It could be from practical training that goes all the way back to my scouting and is still reinforced in my current job. It's as if a hand emerges in my head and rifles through the filing cabinets of my brain, looking for what I need. I know a great deal of it comes from seeing too many of the consequences of danger not foreseen, not handled to someone's utmost. I don't want to be that someone when I could really help.

It did kick in that day, in the dreary hut after a gruelling day that had just become even more so. George and I continued to sweat, jump, press and pant and puff while the young man struggled for life between us.

CHAPTER TEN
SUMMIT PREPARATIONS

WE HUMAN BEINGS ARE not invincible. Yet we live in a death-denying, death-defying society that would have us believe we can outrun, outsmart, outmanoeuvre the demise of anyone. There should be a cure for everything, an answer to every physical dilemma. After all, this *is* the twenty-first century, for heaven's sake. Surely there's a drug, a procedure, a health regime that can restore anyone to wholeness.

As George and I struggled on with the young porter, I couldn't buy into that philosophy.

Still, while we human beings are not invincible, we are incredible in the way we're built, in the way our bodies have the ability to heal themselves under certain circumstances. Our body gives us warnings. If we hurt it's a warning something isn't right. Just like the warning light on a car: keep driving and eventually something serious goes wrong. Pay attention, do what needs to be done and cells regenerate. And that is what slowly happened.

The young man's arms began to move into a more normal shape, away from their rigid, robot-like position.

His eyes gradually came back to life, and he started to smile. He said something – I still have no idea what – I only cared that he was trying to communicate.

And so was I.

Breathless myself, I told George to stop running – and got no complaints from him. I called out for hot tea – well-sugared – and a lot of it. Another coat was found, and I sat the porter down and wrapped him in it. It was a little like the referee in a boxing ring when the fighter has been knocked down, and the ref checks his gloves and sees if he's good to continue the fight.

For the next hour I continually looked him over, asking him to give me a thumbs up or down when I asked how he was feeling, checking his fingers for frostbite and his eyes for signs of life coming back into them and his skin for a colour besides grey. Truthfully, I had no idea what I was looking for beyond that. Maybe just obvious signs he wasn't recovering or was starting to get cold again.

As for his companions, laughter erupted from their corner – not from relief as you might imagine, but from hilarity. Hilarity. I didn't have to comprehend their language to see that they actually found his suffering amusing. To them, this whole thing was a joke – to the point that, as someone translated, they were telling him all he needed to do was just go to the porters' hut.

The porters' hut. I hadn't been through its door, but when it blew open in the wind I could see it wasn't looking much better than ours.

I saw no fire. No hot drinks. Nothing more than a few beds, plastic sheeting and something only barely resembling a blanket to cover him. Within ten minutes he would be right back where he'd started, with no one there to monitor him and get his blood circulating again.

To say I was aghast is an extreme understatement. Clearly no one cared. He was seen as somehow dispensable. But I had to curb my anger. He wasn't out of the woods yet, and an explosion from me was going to do him no good.

Exercising all the control I could summon, I stared at these guys who found this whole event funny.

"There is no way he's going to his hut," I said to them. "He is staying right here where there is some warmth, tea and us. All of you, clear away from the Jiko. I'm sitting him there. He needs it more than you guys." Their eyes protested but I went on. "Yes, we are all cold, but let's get him close and you guys sit near him."

I didn't wait to see how they responded. I directed my attention to our young porter, who was looking at me like a man returning from the dead, which he almost literally was. His colour had come back completely, and his eyes were no longer sinking back into their sockets. His lips, once again alive, turned upward into a small smile. He knew. He knew he'd been in a bad way and we had probably saved him. As he nodded that he was okay, his face was the picture of gratitude. That eased my intolerance of the situation. For the moment.

After he drank a few cups of hot tea and began to have some real life in him, I was happy to give him a little space while I went over our options in my head. Getting him off the mountain right then was not one of them.

That was a two-day hike, and he was far from ready to be exposed to the elements. His going on with the climb was also out of the question. The only real choice was for him to stay put and stay warm. And I didn't much care whether his employer agreed with me.

We all sat down with Enoch and told him – told him, not suggested to him – "This guy is staying here. He's not to go outside. He's to stay here near the warmth, and if he gets cold he is to get moving. And there must be someone here with him."

Enoch never stopped smiling through my entire tirade, and his head bobbed in agreement. Whether he really did see it my way, or he was indicating so to appease me, I'll never know. But our young porter didn't leave the hut that evening.

Away from the other porters, the four of us raised another issue with the smiling Enoch. There is no way, I told him, that you as leaders can bring people up here without proper kit, without checking to make sure they are capable of withstanding these weather conditions. All of us chimed in. Jake said to him, "You've got to look after your staff. You can't put people in this position."

We did it tactfully and carefully because he was, after all, leading us up a mountain, our lives basically in his hands. We didn't want to tick him off – although who could tell with that ... smile. Still, this was no place for complacency. We were talking lives, and no life was worth losing on a mountain that would be there another day. In brief, we laid it all out:

- The porters had totally inappropriate kit for the mountain, nowhere near suitable for the conditions
- The young man very nearly died, and no one seemed the slightest bit concerned
- At the very least, for the credibility of their business, they should conduct checks at the base to make sure people were not climbing up to their deaths. And that included *all* people – not just the customers.

To drive our point home, I said: "Death is a very real prospect. Having experienced that truth recently, I'm not overly pleased about seeing it again."

At last, they took it on board, or they seemed to, anyway. They nodded and agreed that the feedback to make the next group's journey safer was welcomed. By then I was nearing total exhaustion. Man saved, point made. It was time for serious rest.

We were scheduled to leave for the summit in the very early hours of the next morning, and most of my kit was soaked and needed to be dried out by a fire. But at that altitude, with lower oxygen levels and only wet wood to work with, that wasn't going to be easy. First, though, I had to stay curled up in the thin-walled wooden shed with no insulation and try to get the feeling back into my extremities. Even the smouldering annoyance wasn't heating me up.

I left and went into our sleeping room, where I crawled into my sleeping bag just to get some warmth into my feet which, despite my jumping around, were still like blocks of ice in my boots. It was another windy, icy hut to stay in, though it's funny how even that can seem like a small piece of luxury when you're bordering on hypothermia yourself. Still, I had to traverse the pain of moving through 'the cold zone'. That's the zone that exists between fully clothed and warmish to getting undressed and into your thermals for the night. The only thing to do was suck it up and brace myself and make it happen sooner rather than later.

Once I felt like I might have enough energy to get something to eat, I returned to the main hut. The porters had managed to keep the Jiko going and the kettle hot, and they offered some cold, soggy biscuits. I wasn't bothered that they were soggy; I just knew they contained much-needed energy. But the prospect of putting on wet waterproofs and soaked fleece jacket 2 a.m. came was still very real. What I needed were two pairs of thick socks, a thermal base layer, two fleeces and a pair of trousers – all dry – and that wasn't happening.

By then the four of us had all just about reached our limits. We weren't what you would call chatty, and impatience was creeping in. We were hungry, although I had no appetite really. The altitude, the fatigue and a general sick feeling made food, what little there was, unappetizing. I managed to get something down because I knew I was going to need the energy. All of us just focused independently on what we needed to get done, which was to dry our freakin' clothes. Every person there attempted to get a fire going big enough for the job, and by the time someone finally pulled that off, there was only enough time to get our socks and boots from wet to damp.

The one thing that kept me from giving up entirely was, ironically, the weather. The mist was clearing, and the bright sun shone through just like I was on a ski slope, unveiling a display of that mountain – both beautiful and rugged. The air grew still, silent. It was that kind of silence you remember as a kid when you crunched through the snow and spoke almost in reverence – and all the sound was soaked up by the whiteness around you. The sun was high, and I had never appreciated its shine more than I did at that moment.

In four hours, we had walked 10,372 steps – 9 km – and it was suddenly and startlingly worth it. I looked up at the patches of blue I hadn't seen for days and let the relief wash over me. It was all so stunning, even in its harshness, and I thought we were probably going to make it to the top after all. The top, where the real magnificence awaited.

Enoch gathered us for a team briefing, which consisted of telling us we needed to be up at 2 a.m. so we needed to put the crampons on our boots now so we could head up to the summit quickly. That made sense, and I had no problem with it, until he added that we were going to get a lesson on how to climb using ropes. Right there inside the hut. They had a rope tied in the top corner down to the pillar and then, eventually, to us. This was how we were going to practise our rope-climbing skills.

Now, mind you, my sense of humour had all but taken a hike of its own at that point, but I did find that mildly amusing. It was in the let-me-get-this-straight category. We'd gone all that way, were about to attempt to reach the peak – and now they were checking to be sure we knew how to climb? What was this – lastminute.com? Plus, I was physically drained and now I needed to concentrate? I did, only because that sort of thing can save your life or even others from a fall. Still, staring at that wall I said to my friends, "Yeah, that looks exactly like a glacier to me. You?"

We put on our climbing belts and hats and gloves and took up a rope to which an ascender was attached. An ascender is a piece of metal you slide up the rope to arm's length so you can then pull yourself up the rope while using your feet as well to walk up the glacier – or, in this case, the wall. Basically it's a matter of pushing out with your right arm as far as possible so that the small teeth of the ascender can bite into the rope to keep you from falling back down.

We pulled ourselves up again and again in this way ... until we got to the first obstacle (usually where the rope is tied onto an ice screw in the glacier), which is where we had to undo the carabiner from the belt and attach it to the knot that's in the rope by that screw, securing us on the glacier side. Then we removed the ascender past the screw, the obstacle, so we could reattach ourselves safely before removing the carabiner from the fixed point and carrying on.

We did that twice, and it was lesson over. Thankfully, because there were still crampons to be attached to boots, our hard hats to be adjusted to size and our head torches to be attached to them. We also had to fit our climbing belts, which meant stepping into them, looping them around our legs and tightening them at the waist so that all we had to do at zero-dark-thirty was step into them and take off. The preparations still weren't done until we'd attached all the carabiners, screws and all the other small implements we'd need.

My earlier encouraging experience with the sun and the mist notwithstanding, I was now finding the task ahead rather daunting. I was running dangerously low on energy, both physical and mental, and I had to remind myself that we were going to reach the peak at last. I had a vision of what it could look like – without rain, without snow, without hail, and I knew I was going to have to take it all in efficiently, because we had to be up and then down again in very short order.

Yet as much as I tried to look forward to reaching our goal, all the things that had gone wrong stacked up in my head. The unexpected weather. The constantly wet kit. The hunger. The near-death of the young porter and the overall casual lack of concern for him. And, most recently, the bizarre climbing lesson. They were all like voices coming together to shout, "Don't do this! Stop here!"

It would have made perfect sense to do just that. But who wants to be the first to say, "Forget it. I'm not going." When we discussed it later, all three said they would have agreed, thankful that someone had said it. But I didn't. I was a right old mess, yet I didn't feel broken. I felt like I had some more in me.

Yes, everything hurt. Everything was cold. All I wanted to do was stay warm in the sleeping bag. And yet I thought if I didn't have a real excuse not to go on – something along the lines of a broken leg – I couldn't just give up.

The crux of the problem was, and usually is for all of us, that I didn't know how to interpret what was really going on in my head.

On one hand, those thoughts could have been common sense. Looked at objectively, the conditions were not optimum. I didn't really need to have a broken leg to give myself permission to say, "I'm going to call this one and come back another time when conditions are better."

On the other hand, the almost paralyzing doubts could have been the 'demons' speaking. You know, the ones that try to prevent you from accomplishing something. The ones that don't want you to recognize that often life is what waits on the other side of fear. Or the ones that taunt you with, "You're just trying to make things easy. Nothing great ever happened because it was easy."

It was a matter of determining whether to move toward this problem or away from it. To discern whether it was the demon voices or the common sense that were speaking loudest. That was difficult to do with all the factors involved: pride, inconvenience for other people, my own unwillingness to fail.

Yeah. I concluded this was just a tough climb in tough weather. No big deal. Get on with it. My mind was now set. For the moment.

CHAPTER ELEVEN

THANK YOU, WORLD

I DON'T DO THINGS by halves. Normally, I go at everything full tilt – body on the line – and see what happens. So naturally it seemed that the 24th of February, the day we were to reach the peak of Mount Margherita, was a day made for me and my head-on nature. And now that I'd made up my mind, what could stop me?

I was the first to wake up at 2 a.m., and the first to realize how freaking cold it was as my breath turned to mist in the air. The first to shiver my way out of the sleeping bag and change into the layer upon layer of day-time clothes. The clothes were only semi-dry, which made donning them similar to putting on a damp swimsuit. If you've ever had to do that you know how unpleasant it is, but you also know you just have to grin and bear it. Or just bear it.

While my teammates slept on, I stepped outside the small hut and was greeted by the sound of complete and utter nothingness. In that total darkness I met a silence that only comes, as I mentioned earlier, when the snow

127

soaks up even the smallest sound that may have existed. It was eerie, as life is usually a bundle of noise. I was part way up a mountain, nothing stirring, no birds, no wind, no snoring from the huts, no nothing. It was a moment of, "Wow. This is what life can be." I took that moment to gather my thoughts and let them dance around, grateful to be in this soundless environment. Such silence has a power in the focus it gives you. After a few minutes, I thought of nothing, so meditative were those very still minutes.

Soon, the others stirred and emerged from the hut one by one, looking slightly more broken than they had the night before. Faces and shoulders were in various stages of awakeness, and knees were hobbling. Cheeks and chins were unshaven. Skin was lined in pain, as if the journey had gotten into the wrinkles and deepened them. Between that and the various battered-looking get-ups we were all wearing, we resembled a group of Popeyes before the spinach.

Due to the hour, conversation was limited to low mumbles of, "Hello. How you feeling?" and "Food is in there." The only motivating grunts were, "Right. Let's do this," as we made our way to the main hut where the cook was struggling to keep a low-oxygen fire going. The last thing I wanted to do was choke down porridge and highly sugared tea. Whether I was suffering from early altitude sickness or simply sheer exhaustion I wasn't sure, but my appetite had taken a definite hit. I was going to need energy for the day ahead, though, so I gave it a go.

With that done, we put on our hard hats, head torches and climbing belts. Almost the minute I was completely packed into all that stuff, I needed the toilet. I was like the kid whose mum bundles him up in everything from thermals to a snowsuit and he immediately has to use the loo. Off came the kit and off I marched to the mountainside long drop. I had to grope my way to it in the darkness and assume that painful position that my thighs were not a fan of, having been blasted by continuous uphill climbing for days. Seriously, I was burning valuable energy just to relieve myself. It wasn't an auspicious start to the day.

When I rejoined the group, a quick photo was being arranged. The flash didn't work, so the resulting picture showed four shadowy figures standing eerily in the mist. Actually, I found it rather cool, if not downright metaphorical. We truly couldn't see what was ahead of us. We only knew it was there, and despite the fatigue and the bruises and the screaming muscles, there was an air of anticipation. We were finally going to break through that cloud at the 16,000-feet top of Mount Margherita. We were going to accomplish what we'd set out to do. Today. In a few hours.

I didn't have the sizzle of excitement I'd hoped for but, suited up with crampons and a head torch and six layers of clothing on my upper half, three on the lower, I was ready. And I just needed to get going. There is nothing worse than waiting around when you're geared up. I thought but didn't say, Could we just get moving? Let's get the muscles warmed up and move off.

Our spirits were lifted at once by the dry weather. We had only the snow on the ground to contend with, and that continued to provide a peaceful feeling. The early hour was pitch black except for our head torches, and all I could hear was the metal crampon against the snow with the occasional clink on the rock and my own controlled breathing, which was becoming more laboured as the air thinned. At that altitude, you never quite feel that you're getting enough air, so you have to work at it.

Every inhale, every step, was more deliberate than the last as we quietly followed our guides up the rock. I expected all of that. This was the climb we'd all anticipated when we first met at the Urban Eatery in Nairobi and clinked our glasses to reaching the summit. It was so close I could almost smell it.

Our porters may still not have had the proper clothing for this expedition, but the guides did, and they were drilled in kit maintenance. Two of them clutched extra climbing ropes to replace the permanent ropes left on the mountain once we had been up. Their skills made the early stages of the first section of moving uphill uneventful. Our spirits climbed with us. This was it. We were doing this.

And then it all changed.

The first physical challenge was a sixty-degree rope climb of forty feet or more. That doesn't sound far, unless you're at an altitude where your brain is constantly trying to work out whether it's getting enough oxygen. Enoch's brain was clearly functioning as it usually did. The ubiquitous smile accompanied his announcement that there were plenty more of those steep climbs ahead. He seemed to take a fair amount of delight in the dismay on our faces.

Had I expected this kind of challenge? Of course. Margherita Peak is the third highest in Africa. It's 16,795 bloody feet above sea level. What I hadn't expected was to attempt it in my current, physically depleted state, having been essentially beaten up on a daily basis.

But attempt it I did. I told myself that after all the abuse my legs had taken before this, it would be nice to have a change and use my arms. Stepping up to the bottom of the climb, I connected my carabiner clip to the rope and leaned back, the metal figure eight in my right hand, my left guiding the rope away. Our refresher crash course the night before had reminded me to push the figure eight up the rope, guide the rope away as I took a small step with one foot, plant it then follow with the other foot.

First move, fine.

Second move, no problem.

On the third, though, one of my feet gave way and I slipped, landing almost vertically in the snow. I was unhurt, obviously, as the powder was soft as a feather pillow. My ego took a bruising, however, as I picked myself up, reset and started again – only to fall about every third move. It wasn't pretty by any means, and I felt more inept with every slide.

But I kept moving, motivated by the proximity of the top of the rope. When I finally made it, I was fairly pleased with my albeit-chagrined self – only to be welcomed almost immediately by the next rope. Mr Smiley hadn't been kidding. And, by the way, after my delight that my arms would be doing some of the work, they felt like cooked pasta.

I had no choice but to continue the vertical climb, using both arms and legs. I'd have used my sense of humour too, if I'd had one left. It had slipped away about three falls ago, and we were still early on in the climb. We had hours to go yet. I was blowing hard. I knew that I had to keep going but the amount of physical and mental energy needed was massive. Even as I moved upward, I continued to slip – and each time I slipped I knew two things. One, I hadn't made any progress and, two, I'd lost some critical energy. As this went on, the muttering began.

"I can't make it," I said more to myself than to anyone else.

I was told, by Roberts, that of course I could – although I was going to have to move a little faster to catch up.

"No, I'm not doing it," I told him – even while my body kept moving forward as if only it knew that was the right thing to do.

The voices in my brain, however, had other ideas. Take the easy route, they hissed. Take the easy route and stop. They were stuck on repeat: you can't do this – this is too difficult – go back down. The monkey mind is caveman-esque. It's simple. Nothing colourful. No clear directions. It's just a nag, much like the voice that tells you not to invest because you might lose money. It quietly ticks away in your head: don't try out for the lead role because you might be disappointed. In my case, the battle of missions had begun, the monkey mind saying, Let's get him down from here, and me saying, I want to get up ... to the top ... of the mountain.

It wasn't just the physical strain and the mental wrestling that were doing me in. I no longer felt like I was part of a team at that point. Despite the presence of the guides and the cognitive awareness that the other three guys weren't far above, I felt very much on my own. I couldn't see them through the mist, and that was playing havoc with my mental state. I couldn't escape the same sense I had in the Nairobi mortuary, moving in a channel of focus through a cacophony of noise. It created an element of loneliness, of vulnerability. If I just stop, will anyone notice? Or will they just keep going as long as I mind the rope?

The wind was taunting me, howling as it tortured my face. The routine of plant the foot, slip, replant continued to burn precious energy, and even the realization that I wasn't the only one this was happening to didn't make it any easier. For every one step I attempted, I ended up taking two, which was quickly destroying my love affair with this mountain. In fact, I was actually beginning to hate the whole ordeal.

And what about the guides? Oh, Roberts, Ochora and Enoch were there, close enough to shout advice through the wind. But, virtually starving and feeling weak as a dead fish, the last thing I wanted to hear was, "Just step there. Now step here." The instruction that finally did me in was Enoch saying, "Now, mind the rope there as you step."

That was the end of my mental rope. I turned on him and his blasted smile and shouted, "I couldn't give a fuck about your rope!"

I didn't look at him long enough to see if he kept smiling.

Yeah, this whole thing was what can only be described as pure trudge. I wasn't thinking about the view to come or the sense of accomplishment I was going to feel when I reached the top. My body was knackered. I was a wreck. My thighs were on fire, and my muscles didn't seem capable of another step without excruciating pain. I was practically in flames on the inside yet almost frozen on the outside.

We'd been through horrific moments, even hours, on this trip, but they were nothing compared with this. They were all culminating in a waking nightmare of ice and pain and exhaustion and frustration. By then, I didn't have the energy to proclaim that I couldn't make it. I'd used that up on Enoch and his rope. I tried to slow everything down and focus on my next step and my next, concentrating on planting my foot to secure a grip and then move slowly upwards.

But a deepening weakness made that difficult, as did the fact that normally I would have been stepping into the footprints of the person in front of me, making the grip more efficient. Jake, in front of me, was disrupting and destabilizing the snow, making any step I took even more difficult.

By then all I wanted to do was move faster so I'd get to the peak more quickly and it would finally be over. However, slow going was the wiser choice – I needed to proceed with a deliberate patience I didn't feel.

Breathing was beyond difficult. I felt as if I was stuck in an enclosed space in which everyone was competing for the small amount of oxygen available. The higher we climbed, the more I struggled. The air was so thin I could no longer think straight, and there was no overpowering the monkey-mind voices. They became louder and more powerful. *Just sit here and freeze to death. Seriously, give up. Let the mountain take you. It's beaten you. It has won. Just say thank you to the world and be done with it.* Then silence. No wind. No cold. No voices. No clinking of the metal climbing gear. Just peace, warmth, and silence. I had said thank you to the world and I was gone.

But something else was stronger; something I didn't call up myself but which was very suddenly there in brilliant colour. As clichéd as it may sound, I could clearly see moving pictures of my past life flashing before me. Getting married. Having kids. Even childhood events. All those things were rushing past.

And then it all slowed down and stopped. I was on the front row of my own cinema watching my two daughters and me in big, loud, technicolour film.

And there before me, as real as reality itself, was Sunday Fight Night.

I could see the red sofa in our lounge when I was still married and my daughters Imogen and Arabella were young. I could see me sitting there on that red sofa – and then I was on that sofa, with my two little girls who had big, scheming smiles on their faces. They were ready for the fights. I was actually back on that couch after a roast dinner and pudding – cuppa tea in hand. As soon as my cup was emptied and placed on the side, those two very excited little girls edged closer and closer to me. I could smell them. Sense their warm little bodies. One took the sofa route and one the floor, and as they got within launching distance they screamed, "Daddy, it's Sunday Night Fight Night!"

Amid squeals and little-girl laughter, they launched themselves at me like small missiles. Having absolutely no choice whatsoever in the matter, I joined them in rough and tumble at its finest. No hard blows here, just soft wrestling, head rolls.

There on the mountain, where moments before I had been ready to cash in life entirely, I was not only seeing all of this play out – I was reliving it. I was on the face of a glacier, blasted by extreme cold and dangerous loneliness, and yet I was not. I was with my kids, feelings whizzing around and within me.

Back in those days the girls were about 7 and 5. Now they are 20 and 18, but to me they are always 7 and 5. They were those small girls at that moment on the mountainside and, oddly, a poem came to mind. It was one Arabella had given to me years before, and whose author is unknown. Whoever that poet was, they spoke to me clearly as I hung on.

What Is a Dad?

A dad is someone who
Wants to catch you before you fall
But instead picks you up
Brushes you off,
And lets you try again

A dad is someone who
Wants to keep you from making mistakes
But instead lets you find your own way,
Even though his heart breaks in silence
When you get hurt

A dad is someone who
Holds you when you cry
Scolds you when you break the rules
Shines with pride when you succeed,
And has faith in you even when you fail ...

I was a dad before I began the climb, but the monkey mind was convincing me that in that place on that mountain at that time, I was nothing. In truth, I was reduced to needing a dad, and there was none. There was no father to hold me as I was fighting for life. I had only the voices in my head, trying to take me down.

At that point, even in the midst of the Fight Night movie, the demons were in charge. I could hear them on the wind deriding and mocking me: Those children? You'll never see them again. Those Sunday Night Fight

Nights? They are never going to happen again. No more Imogen. No more Arabella. You have failed.

I was literally in tears. In fact, those tears were the only thing I could feel on my frozen face.

Having such deep, dark thoughts was a first for me. I had seen and smelled death many times. I was literally immersed in it after the hotel attack in Nairobi and had faltered more than once seeing bodies and bits of bodies, watching the abject grief of families, but I'd ploughed through it. This was on a completely different level – a far deeper level. I was the one facing death this time. I was at the bottom and for me there was no route up, down or out. I couldn't do anything. The demon voices had become like a marching band, blaring through and drowning out every positive thought I might have had, every forward action I could have taken.

Actually, I wasn't even thinking, How do I suppress them? How do I defeat them? How do I negotiate with them? I was overcome by them as they took control of me, of my mind and my actions: This is it. This is the end. These demons have won. It was a surreal, out-of-body experience.

But we have a choice, and many of us only make a choice on whatever is causing us stress when we know what is enough. When we know to say: I'm not standing for this any more. That's when we decide to end the relationship, get down to the gym, book a holiday or just do what we have always wanted to do. Even with the demon tubas blaring around me, I knew I had a choice whether to sit there and let the wind blow through me and grow colder and colder and colder until I stopped living.

But there was no way. I'd hit the bottom. I'd had enough of the voices. My choice was right there in the darkness that followed my 'film', and with an out-loud exclamation, littered with swear words, I cried out, "No! I'm getting back down from this mountain, back to my life, back to my daughters and our Sunday Night Fights. Ff&* you, demons!"

What followed was a reframe of that Fight Night video, from playing our rough and tumble on the red sofa to a taunt to the death demons and into the motivation to get me off the ground and up the mountain. I did what we're all capable of in those rock-bottom moments, even if we don't believe it. I visualized those closest to me but, more than that, this new video was a future image with me fairly and squarely in it.

I saw me loving them, saw them in the best times, during the best experiences. Painting that moving picture reminded me what I had was important, and what I was doing right then was significant as well. I closed my eyes and intensified the imagery, making it so immensely powerful that I rose like a phoenix. Nothing BUT NOTHING was going to stand in the way of me getting back to those girls.

Straight on the back of that, I dug out the video of me at the top of this mountain, hands aloft as if I'd won a race, smiling and shouting, "Yes!" I could see how amazing it was, how I'd overcome fears and hardships. How I had become pure mental and physical toughness. And as

I watched that film play out, I heard only the words: You are good enough.

I had never pushed myself as hard as I did when we – the guides, the porters, my teammates and I – moved from there across the glaciers towards Margherita Peak. It was snowing again, heavily, which made visibility awful. Fresh snow meant slipping feet. Increasing lack of oxygen caused a fight with confusion. Sheer torture created unbelievable pain. But my feet were still fine. That was something. And so I pushed on with the others.

Speaking of the others, I was not the only one who was frustrated and discouraged. Big, hearty George was looking as if he'd been beaten with a club, and he trudged with his shoulders hunched in defeat. We weren't really speaking to each other, not because we didn't care enough to ask, "You all right?" Each of us was simply so focused on taking one step at a time in that final climb.

Which was the worst.

"We have a narrow ledge coming up," Enoch told us.

That was the definition of an understatement.

The ledge in question was not only narrow – no wider than a foot – it was made of solid ice, formed only a few days earlier by the freezing rain and plummeting temperatures. In order to make our way beneath the admittedly beautiful stalactites that had formed – looking like the lovely feathers of birds – we had to crouch, while carrying an ice axe, which replaced the ropes we couldn't use in that situation.

Basically, at six-feet-one, I had to make myself three-feet-three to traverse the ledge and round the corner. Picture edging along an outside windowsill around the top-most point of a skyscraper, an iced sill at that, and you will have something of a sense of what it was like.

Both the demons' voices and my own you-can-do-this message had been replaced by Holy FUCK! This ledge I speak of hung out over nothing. If we slipped, we were done. There was nothing to catch us or break our fall. We wouldn't survive. If the ice broke, our only chance was to hold on to the ice axe planted in the sheer face of the rock, and even that was iffy. That axe was made for, well, ice, not solid stone.

One at a time we moved round, with all the tall guys having to reduce themselves down and creep round, trusting life to an ice axe, a new ice shelf and a big dose of guts. Somehow we all made it and stopped to gather our breath, each of us still roped to one other person. We didn't speak much. We were focused. This was not the time for jokes. No sooner had relief begun to surge in than Enoch informed us there was yet another one, even narrower than its predecessor. I let go with an elongated Are. You. Kidding. Me?

There was nothing for it but to make our way extreme-ly slowly, which we did, this time without ice axes, along a narrow ledge no wider than our feet and against a ver-tical icy wall of rock. Below us? Nothing. The sheerest of nothingness. It was worse than the previous one. It re-quired precision foot placement. It required us to face the wall and lean into it as we traversed across. Knowing we had dumped the ice axes, I knew we also needed to come back this way. Yeah, the joys just kept mounting. Meanwhile, the wind was sandblasting our faces with heavy snow. But we had to go for it. Hesitation would have been deadly.

When we finally stopped at the far end of that four-metre-long ledge, my jacket was soaked in snow, adding to the weight, and I felt it in the burning pain in my arms, my thighs, my lungs. We paused. There was another rope climb to navigate. Up we went over thin ice on rock, giving new meaning to the word 'trudging'.

None of us really knew where we were, where we were going, or even if we were close. We had to be, or I believed Michiel truly was not going to make it. The hulking Dutchman, every bit as in shape as any of the rest of us, was breathing in a rapid, laboured way that was truly frightening. This was not just the altitude – it was an exhausted human being struggling for air.

But we continued to plod. We had no choice, really. All sense of a goal had been lost ... and then BOOM, a white sign, almost obliterated by snow:

WELCOME TO MARGHERITA PEAK
5,109 METERS ABOVE SEA LEVEL
"THE HIGHEST POINT IN UGANDA"

The sign just seemed to arise out of nowhere, telling us we'd made it. I thought we still had a long way to go, but I had arrived. I had convinced my brain I would get there, and I had. It was by far my most emotional moment yet. Relief, joy, amazement and tears all ran together. I wanted to collapse onto my knees and hold my head in my hands.

The porters had a different reaction. "This weather is crazy," they said to us. They, like myself and my teammates, were nothing short of shattered, physically and mentally. And yet they said, repeatedly, "You are so strong."

Little did they know. Because this wasn't over.

CHAPTER TWELVE

LET'S GET OFF THIS MOUNTAIN

IT DOESN'T STOP when you get to the top.

Ask anyone you know who has achieved a dream. Maybe the owner of a business she dreamed of starting, or the person who summoned up the courage to apply for that job he thought he wasn't good enough for. Look into the life of a person you idolize or follow who has reached the pinnacle in his or her field. How does it feel to be 'there?' you'll ask. If that person is honest, the answer will be: 'There' is where the real work starts.

The problem with that truth is that it's so unexpected. After the hard work it takes to even get to the start line, not to mention to the halfway point and finally to that peak, finding out that's when the hard part really begins can be demoralizing. That happened to me on the summit of that mountain.

We'd reached the peak of Margherita. All those days of physical misery and mental anguish had taken us to the top. I could enact my vision of raising my arms to the heavens and proclaiming I had made it. It was supposed to be a moment of celebration, a moment of joy.

Yeah. I took a video there and, yes, indulged in a few moments of celebration. But in the film I am heard to say, rather starkly, "This will probably be my last video." I didn't mean my last video of the trip. I meant my last video ever. I had brought my vision to life through an awesome achievement, but the voices were back in my head saying: I don't want to continue.

I'm quite serious when I say that I was considering testing out that medical insurance I'd purchased, although it didn't cover the last 400 feet … Couldn't I just break an ankle or a leg and be helicoptered down? Or why not simply throw myself off the highest peak in the Rwenzori? What was the best way to get out of this?

It's fair to say the demons will try to own you, even – or perhaps especially – when you've reached a goal you've put body, mind and soul into attaining. They will come for you, try to take control of you. Their showing up, however, is not the end of it.

It's time to thank them.

I'm not joking. Thank them for their gift of motivation. No matter what they say, take it, thank them and kick their ass. There's nothing they like less than your success.

I had to show the demons. It was time to bring back that powerful, motivating movie image: Sunday Fight Nights. That positive, strengthening voice managed to whisper its way in; the same voice that had kept me from letting go before I saw myself and my daughters in the marvellous throes of our weekend wrestling matches. It was the voice that said: I've got this. I am strong. I am loved. I have reached the top, and I am amazing.

I had a choice right then, before we began our descent. I could fight those demons until they won and tossed me over the 16,000-feet side to certain death. Or I could simply turn from them and believe the softer voice. The true voice.

While the decision might appear easy, I was physically far too unwell to step right into it. All of us were. It had taken us six hours to reach the top that day, and, to a man, we were broken. Broken and frozen George was shivering so hard he was nearly convulsing. Michiel's breathing was alarmingly short, sharp and shallow. Jake was silent. I found out later from a mutual friend that he texted his wife, gushing emotion. Not his M.O. at all.

We had snacks with us, but I didn't eat because I knew, if I did, I would throw it all up. I was dehydrated. The wind had burned my face raw. Sweat was dripping from my nose, stinging my chapped, open skin with its salt. All of our clothes were soaked from perspiration and the elements.

First, just get me off this thing, my own voice told me. So I followed the others in a descent down the mountain, determined and focused. This was no time to switch off. More concentration than ever was required, because complacency is the mother of many mistakes.

There really wasn't much danger of that. Clearly, conditions hadn't changed just because we made it to the top. Just as we'd done on the way up, we slipped and slid over the icy rocks, back down the ropes, down sixty degrees of steep. Granted, being roped together made our way back across those narrow ice ledges seem somewhat easier the second time. We crossed and climbed glaciers and sheer walls of ice. In the clean, crisp air, we hiked, hiked and continued to hike, until I finally broke out the food – just a little, sweet snack to keep me going. Simply being able to bring myself to put anything in my mouth was a small victory.

As we continued down the glaciers, we hoped to catch a glimpse of the view. Finally, in one sudden moment, the clouds opened, and we could see the beautiful blue-grey mountain ranges rising mystically from the clouds, the glistening snow and ice and, in the very far distance, the low slopes of greenery. I'd envisioned this stunning view all the way up. A spot of joy at last as I actually gazed on it.

But that joy was fleeting. We were still trying to make our way over glaciers and ledges and all the other dangers that had tried to take us out on the way up. And through it all, Enoch continued to smile. I was starting to hate that grin, to be honest. When he told me for the fiftieth time not to stand on his rope ...

"I don't give a monkey's about your rope," I said, teeth clenched. "And if you carry on with that advice, I will chuck you off this mountain myself."

I was only partly joking. But staying upright and focusing on the task was just pipping the importance of his rope. Okay, so for him the rope was vital, and, after all, he was correct in that it could save someone's life in the future. Maybe it was just that damn grin.

As we continued down, the snow also continued. I was constantly losing my grip, and my feet spent more time slipping than actually meeting the rock. I planted my right foot onto the snow, and it slipped forwards a few feet, while I took the next step with my left to gather myself. I slipped and slid down that mountain concentrating only on staying upright.

We battled on for hours and hours until we made it to the more familiar low slopes. We edged our way down the rocks, tired and weary bodies stretched to the limits, reaching down with a foot but not quite making it the floor, using a hand on a rock face to steady our drop. Then off we stepped, a short drop down to the next rock as a shudder ran through the body. The routes were wet and narrow, some so much so we had to squeeze through, others that forced us to sit down and slide. Whatever way we chose didn't have to look impressive. It just had to limit the impact.

And then, like a mirage, huts appeared in the distance. For a moment I was boosted by that, mentally, but with every step I took, they only seemed to remain forever far from us. There was no way we were actually getting closer to them. By that time, the slipping was less a factor of the ice and rock and more my inability to jump from one boulder to another. There was no chance that I'd actually make it without falling or twisting something. Bizarre as, not long before, I was quite happy to test out that medical insurance.

Eventually the huts of the Margherita Camp did get closer until we were there, welcomed by food. But, again, I couldn't immediately face it for fear of chucking it all back up. And there was a decision to make. After a brief rest we could carry on for another three hours to the lower camp, or we could stay at the Margherita until tomorrow. But that would make for quite a long hike the next day, and none of us was sure we were up to it.

Personally, I knew I needed a sleep before I decided. I hadn't slept well the night before our final ascent, and to say it had been a difficult day on every level would be to grossly understate the facts. Even a short rest period would help. Otherwise, I wasn't going to make it.

I went to the hut, had a quick change and lay down with my legs propped up. I had a small carton of juice and, while lying on my back, I raised my head off the floor, just enough to drink. This position was the only thing I could think of to drain some of the lactic acid from my muscles.

An hour passed. I thought maybe I'd fallen asleep, but it was hard to tell because my whole body was a bit stiff. I very carefully swung my legs downwards, lay on my side and let the blood reach all the extremities before I lifted my aching, battered body off the floor. Now I really did have to make a decision: stay in Margherita or summon the energy to get down to Huntsman's Camp.

I joined the others, and we discussed the matter. Three out of four of us decided to head down. With more oxygen at that level, there would be a better fire, and we would have a shorter walking day the next day. The one who opted to stay was Michiel.

Our strong, strapping Dutch compadre was physically shattered. Beaten up by the weather and the toil, he looked completely dishevelled – hair wild on his head, eyes sunken, much like the young porter George and I had saved. His feet in particular were practically in shreds. And that was just his physical state. Slumped on his bed, inside his sleeping bag, he wasn't for moving. At all. The only word I could use to describe him was 'forlorn'. He was almost at the edge, and for him to continue on another step that day was out of the question.

So the question was, Now what? And there was only one answer. We had to leave him behind. I'd never done that before, and after what we had just been through, I wasn't keen on doing it now, even though he promised to join us the next morning. A team is a team, and breaking it apart reduces everyone's resilience.

Two of the porters did stay with him, and we made sure he had food and some warmth, though the latter was minimal. Michiel himself assured me he would be fine, that we were over the worst. He just needed rest, and he'd be perfectly okay after some decent sleep.

By then it was already 4 p.m., and we needed to get going. Having an hour's sleep and a small, cold chapati and egg, the rest of us tracked down the hill. Actually, 'track' is a bit of an exaggeration. In those wellington boots, we were careening on snow, sliding on ice-covered rocks and fighting the melted ice streams being created around us. The sun was out, which turned the snow to slush and made the going even more treacherous. There was no getting purchase with our feet; it was one long, precarious toboggan, minus the fun. We just needed to get to the end of it before darkness set in.

I have to say that although my whole body was still screaming at me for causing it so much pain, my legs were sturdier than they'd been earlier. Maybe the raised legs thing had worked. I didn't care what the reason was. At least I could plough on.

Psychologically, the going was rough as well. We were supposedly headed down the mountain, away from all that. But we were continually going up in the very midst of the descent. That zigzag pattern was beyond demoralizing. It was mentally destructive. I wanted this. Over. With.

Finally ... the welcome sight of the camp on the ridge. It was still some distance away. There was the swamp to go through along the river and the final short-but-steep climb to the camp to manage. But the difference in the oxygen levels and the fact we could see the huts on the edge of the precipice made all the difference.

So did the brief Wet Wipes wash I immediately gave myself when we arrived. And the change of clothes. And the wood-burner with its roaring fire. If we hadn't just been through virtual hell, this would have been called 'roughing it'. To me it was the Ritz London.

I was so completely knackered, I wasn't sure what I craved first – food or water or rest. I opted for water and coffee with the guides around the wood-burner while we dried out our clothes. I was dazed and tingling as I mentally and privately recounted the moments I had experienced on that mountainside. None of it had meaning for me yet. I simply played through the events in my mind and took a quick look back through some of the photos I'd taken. It seemed as if I had just been in another world.

Only then did I focus on the one thing I knew had been ravaged by the elements – my face. It was so completely raw from the wind and cold that when I touched it, I felt disconnected from it, as if I weren't making contact with it at all. It was that wretched thing that happens when you have a prolonged cold and your nose gets red and tender from wiping it – all the way from your nostrils to your upper lip. This, however, covered my entire face. I smothered it in Vaseline and drank water, hoping to re-hydrate while we chatted.

The guides and George and Jake and I didn't talk about anything heavy. The experience was still too naked and vulnerable to be sorted through in a group. We discussed the drying of the clothes and the awesomeness of the hypnotic fire, and slowly I began to feel somewhat reattached. That final day had left me isolated, alone with my demons, and simply to have company and oxygen and shelter and warmth made me feel far less alone in the struggle I'd experienced. Or in the struggle that lay ahead for me to deal with.

We had dinner – a mountain of food prepared by an excellent cook. By then I was ready to eat, and to be honest, I would have eaten a rabid dog between two bread vans. Still, I forked the food in wearily, fuel that we just needed to consume, though not too fast. We had to treat that whole eating thing with a certain amount of gentleness.

Very few words were spoken. Instead, as we dined together, I observed our guides, and my ideas about them softened. In spite of everything, they did get us to the top. And down. Despite the beyond-annoyances and the lack of safety – and Enoch's maddening smile – he and Ochora and Roberts had led us quite magnificently through some horrific conditions. They were strong men, and I had to give credit where it was due.

I woke up the next morning having not rested well at all, again, in spite of the welcome warmth of my sleeping bag. My sinuses were raw and swelling, my head banging. Some kind of infection was brewing. The fact that the temperature was still freezing didn't help.

But there were saving graces. Our clothes were dry. Another blazing fire greeted us in the main hut, which had probably been going all night. Best of all, the pain in my face notwithstanding, I felt a huge grin spread over it when I spotted Michiel, walking along the boardwalk on the lower hillside below us. We could track him as he moved closer and closer, and it was hard not to full-out cheer when I realized he was actually bounding along, body straight, the way we were accustomed to seeing him.

When Michiel arrived, he entered the hut, full of beans, as we say, and announced how great he felt. He'd just needed that rest. He'd had a small cereal bar and some rice at Margherita Camp, there being no fire there to cook, and he must have gotten up before dawn to join us that early. But the human spirit is clearly indomitable, and he was ready to be with us for our descent by 10 a.m. After he wolfed down breakfast.

Ever the optimist, Enoch offered us the option of climbing another peak en route, or using the easier route, which was over the Bamwanjara Pass – at 14,000 feet. We chose the latter. If I'd had to manage another peak I might actually have hurled myself off it. Although, we weren't fifteen minutes into it before I wondered, if this was the 'easier route', what must the harder one have been like? Forget the generous thoughts I'd had about him the night before. This guy was trying to kill us.

There we were again, trekking up as many steep inclines as we trekked down. Up and over boulders. In the streams running off the mountain. My legs were on fire. The bottoms of my wellington boots had become as thin as my patience. As I said, my positive feelings about our guides the night before had vanished, and I was cursing under my breath.

We finally did make it over Bamwanjara Pass. We had a very quick lunch at the top – it was windy as hell – and I could only stomach an apple and some juice, passing on the dried potato salad sandwich that had been hanging around for a week in the worst weather on the planet. Who eats that any time? I fancied something juicy and wet, and there was none of that. I was actually glad to get back onto the three steps down, two steps up trail again, just to put the whole thing behind me. Every step wrung out my body.

Along the way, Enoch was giving us time estimates for our arrival at the camp – estimates that fluctuated wildly.

We stopped at the helicopter pad so Michiel could tend to his feet, which were still in tatters, being held together with tape. We waited for him; there was no leaving anyone this time. At that point, Enoch said we didn't have far to go.

After we sloshed across the swamp toward a small stream that had broken its bank, we had to do a quick think about whether we should jump, wade or find a route across. I was just on the cusp of making it, but with tired legs and a less-than-good surface to take off from, we decided we didn't need to get soaked, which would have happened if we misjudged. We found a way across that required just a short, easily doable jump, and then we were off again. Time estimate: not far to go. How could that possibly be?

We continued through the shrubs of the smaller but sharp hills, which were real lung-beaters. They made me realize who was in charge on this mountain, and it wasn't us. At that juncture, Enoch announced that the camp was at the bottom of a massive rock we could see in the wide white valley below us. The rock was an obelisk, the perfect symbol for arrival. I understood the meaning of the phrase, Take heart.

From there we crossed massive waterfalls, the crashing sound of which no photograph can capture. We carried on, tracking down for another hour and a half over rugged terrain comprised of boulders and submerged tree roots. It was, shall we say, unpleasant. In fact, it occurred to me that if we had been in Europe making this trip, we would never have made it to the top because the whole thing would have been cancelled due to the danger. But at last we made it to the bottom of that longed-for obelisk of a rock.

There was no camp there.

I felt like Enoch was just leading us with a carrot dangling from a string at the end of a stick, and I was not pleased. I won't assault you with the words I hurled. Among ourselves the wit was sharp. "Don't tell me, Enoch, let me guess – it's just over that hill – and that one – and that one."

We still had to walk down a horrific hillside caught between two massive rock faces, which meant we were constantly in cold, wet shade. The jumps we had to make from boulder to boulder were nearly vertical, making it necessary to use ropes and even trees just to navigate. Enoch kept talking about "the path", but I was not convinced there was one, and if there was, this wasn't it. Every step in those flimsy wellington boots was like being stabbed in the soles of the feet.

Do I even have to explain why those dark thoughts of wanting to use that medical insurance surfaced again? Let me just snap a bone. Let someone else carry me. I am broken.

Somehow we made it to the base camp, Kibaro, which was still at a high altitude. My nose was burning, and all I could imagine was the tip of it turning black and dropping off. The only thing that tore that image from my mind was the upscale quality of the camp. Everything is, after all, relative. There were wooden huts and bunk beds and a large dining area and, heaven, standard long-drop toilets that were a whole lot less leg-torturing than the ones we'd had to deal with before.

But it was probably the setting that immediately began to heal me. The sounds of the river. Birds chattering among themselves. Green trees. Fresh smells. Even a clearing that called for a picnic and a country walk amid the welcome greenery. I parked myself in the sunshine and savoured a scene that wasn't threatening to kill me.

Dinner was a meat stew with potatoes and butternut squash, made by a cook with a talent for putting a meal together, but I still had no appetite. I forced it down for energy reasons. As soon as supper was over, I went straight to bed. The next day was to be our last on that mountain.

As I lay there resting and waiting for sleep, I let my thoughts travel forward – to being in some sort of civilization where there was decent food I'd have an appetite for, and a warm, comfortable bed I could sink into. I imagined hearing Karen's voice, and those of my children. I could see and hear all those things because I knew them.

But something not so familiar was already seeping in. It was just a small sense, but it was there. Although I was returning to the same life I had left, I had somehow changed. I just didn't know how much.

That was still to come.

CHAPTER THIRTEEN

A WHOLE NEW WORLD

MY SENSES WERE completely filled up.

That's not something that happens to most of us in modern civilization. We're used to having them clogged with pollution and noise and over-salted fast food. It has become such a way of life we don't even realize we're not truly feeling, not fully experiencing. In essence we are walking around half-alive.

But the morning I awoke for our final descent to Kilembe, every sense was stimulated to its max capacity.

The sun was coming up atop the dense forest that surrounded us. Birds were greeting us with songs that rivalled the London symphony – and definitely exceeded the music pouring from someone's phone. Although even that sounded brighter and crisper than I ever remembered.

It was the air itself that intoxicated me, though. It was so clear, so sweet, I could almost taste it. I had that no-pain sensation you get when you come out of IV sedation. Know what I mean? At once invigorating and calming, as

159

if all things are now possible. In short, I could breathe again, and I was convinced air was something we can't truly appreciate until we've been without it.

Even amid the hustle of packing for that last day, the mood was upbeat. Despite the heat and humidity, we all seemed to be moving lightly. We still had a full day to tackle, and were under no illusion that it was going to be a breezy path downhill. But we'd seen the worst, and we were filled with the best nature had to offer.

After a quick photo shoot with the guides and porters, we were off, sunscreen applied and hats on. Of course, the downward progress came with what seemed like upward loss of progress, but I was used to that by then. Nothing seemed to be able to bring down our buoyant spirits. There was almost a party atmosphere. Sure, people's feet were taped up, and we were more than a little worse for wear, but none of that could compare to what we'd already been through.

I had more time in those last hours to observe the crew again. The guides were confident, sure-footed – and nobody was telling me to mind the bloody rope. The porters were still making it in only flimsy wellington boots and doing so without complaint. This was a tough group. I'd learned more from them than I realized.

The further down we climbed, the more wildlife we saw. The red velvety deer were my personal favourites. Called duiker, they're sort of a stocky but small antelope found only in the Rwenzori. Like most deer-like creatures, they're skittish and scared, and they disappear into the undergrowth the moment they sense a threat. And apparently everything is a threat. Not a fun way to live, I imagine.

I, on the other hand, felt afraid of nothing at that point. Between the never-silent trilling birds and the thick greenery that bordered our path on both sides, I was fearless as we knocked off the kilometres. My big toes were warm, and I knew I was in a pre-blister situation, but after all the pain and misery of the past days, it felt good to focus on something so small and so fixable.

The hilarious – at least to us – conversations we'd carried on in our first few days together resumed. All four of us were jokers of a sort; mine being the lowest form of humour. My sarcasm is such that even close friends will say they're never quite sure whether I'm joking or not. When the path completely disappeared into the underbrush at one point, I said to our guide, "You take this path a lot, do you?" Fortunately, he got the humour in stating the complete and utter obvious, because there were still plenty of opportunities for him to let me tumble over the side.

We stopped for lunch on a rocky overhang by the river where porters from below had arrived ahead of us and started a cook fire. It was as close to a sidewalk cafe as I had been in over a week. Seated on benches at an actual table, we tucked into chips, fresh coleslaw and tomatoes while watching the entertainment: the porters and guides diving into the water with a bar of soap.

This was the chance I'd been wanting to really dwell on the river and its roar as it rushed downhill. I thought of how good it would feel to be a water molecule. Hear me out – I wasn't losing it. I wondered about the experience of being that one mysterious combination of oxygen and hydrogen, taking all those risks over rocks and down the sides of boulders, just to use the most efficient route in one direction, with none of the ups and downs we were having to contend with.

I took the risk thing even further. Any one of those molecules could be used up by a plant or an animal. But maybe that was the challenge of life: dodging through the risks to end up in the freedom of the big, wide ocean. That may seem an odd series of thoughts to have at that point, but in hindsight I see the effects of the treacherous journey I'd just been on were already taking hold. It was my first indication that the mind I climbed up the mountain with was not the same one I possessed going down. I just didn't fully know it at the time.

Not long after lunch we reached a crossroads, which gave us two options. One route would take only ninety minutes but promised to be very hard on the knees. The other would use up two hours yet would be what the guides called "a nice walk". No one answered at first, so I led the way with a lean toward making things easier. Two hours of nice probably wouldn't take the full two. Why not be comfortable at this point?

No one else had wanted to say it, but they seemed glad I did. Seriously, there was nothing left to prove.

The guides were not wrong. It was a delightful hike. The cricket noise was like a washing machine in for a spin. The avian life was in full song, and we even caught sight of monkeys swinging among the high branches and chattering to each other. No one has as much fun as a bunch of primates, truly.

We marched down in an almost spritely fashion, keen to get to the ranger's hut, which we did, to sign out of the wildlife zone and back into the community. It was like nothing more than coming out of Jurassic Park, a place where no one goes. I felt as if I was leaving an entirely different world behind. The sense of relief as we came down the last hill into even more oxygen and greenery was elating.

As we walked down the final hillside we could see the valley open up. In the dazzling sunshine and beneath pristine blue skies were beautiful views of rolling country-side. As we drew closer to the village we passed a school. Kids sitting in their ill-fitting, raggedy clothes watched us and smiled and waved. Teachers chatted nearby, while others sat in the shade out of the burning sun. While we had been up the mountain experiencing life as it had never been before, they'd been continuing with lives that would probably never change.

We headed further down into the village, past the basic, baked-brick houses, past the junior school. On the roadside, mums bent forward over their stock of vegetables for sale, whipping away flies. Dads, chilling, lay on the ground watching the world go by. The odd cow and some goats roamed while many chickens clucked and pecked, avoiding being dinner.

In the town of Kasese itself – a busy T-junction just like you would imagine in a Western film – food and drink were being served, and people were riding bikes with their crops of bananas balanced on the back. A church was belting out hymns through slightly crackly speakers at a volume that was just too much. At a bank cash point, armed guards stood outside, preoccupied with checking their phones.

It was not the life I was used to, but it was far closer than the terrain I'd just returned from. And yet it didn't feel at all familiar. There was something different I couldn't shake off. I didn't know then that I never would.

Once on the other side of that last chain-link fence, we passed what were now more recognizable sights. The coffee and avocado plantations. The young kids waving and cheering as if we'd just arrived from some great mission, which I supposed six days in the Rwenzori is. Some of the children high-fived us as we passed, and although it was clear they thought we were stupid wazungu for even doing such a thing, I decided to take it as "Well done!"

When we arrived at the front door of the Rwenzori Trekking Services office – that same door we'd passed through before we started – it seemed like a lifetime ago. My mind went straight to all the wonderfully mundane things I hadn't considered in six days: the sofas in the reception area and four large Nile beers.

That was where we sat, beers in hand, while we completed our feedback forms, worked out the tip, and thanked the guides and porters. At that point I wished I hadn't burned my down jacket, but I did have a thermal base layer, and I had a plan for it: the young porter who had carried my bag all the way up to Margherita and all the way down in clothes you'd wear on a spring walk down to the shops. I gave him that thermal base layer, and he thanked me with such huge smiles and so much humility I was humbled myself. Most of us wouldn't do any kind of work for five dollars an hour, much less five dollars a day. He and his fellow porters had risked their lives in brutal conditions at that pay rate. I wished I had more to give him.

In my feedback form I said they were all fantastic, and they were, really. I also wrote – adamantly – about the porters needing better kit. If I was going to leave one thing behind it was that. One more porter should not be brought to the brink of death.

We all thanked our crew personally as well, first the porters and then the guides, which was the established pecking order. To my surprise, they reciprocated with praise, especially Enoch. Maybe they tell everyone this, but they said we were some of the strongest people they had ever taken up the mountain. They said they'd seen many people turn back in less savage conditions than those we'd encountered. I bit my tongue to keep from asking, Seriously? That was a choice?

The bigger surprise was the certificate each of us received, certifying that we had completed the trek. That in itself wasn't unexpected, but these were quite snazzy, with our names beautifully written out on good stock paper. I've received dozens of awards in my time, but this was the most hard-fought-for one I'd ever been given. There were blood, sweat and tears in that thing, and it meant more to me than the group photo or the high-fiving. Or Enoch's last grin. There was real meat in it, and that caught me off guard.

How did I feel about the entire experience at that point? I was physically broken. Hot. Sweaty. Legs on fire. And my kit had taken a bashing. All I could think at that moment was that I never wanted to see another mountain again. I never wanted to see my gear again, for that matter, and in fact what I didn't give away I abandoned. That was how done I was.

Soon after, the taxi arrived for us, with the same driver who had dropped us there a little less than a week before. I was struck by how fresh he looked, how clean the cab was. That was probably because, after six days without bathing, we smelled nothing less than rotten. It was in that state that we made our way out of the tin mining village, with its chickens and goats and little kids in the street, and slowly back into civilization.

As the road grew bumpier, we came to that place where previous flooding had brought down boulders the size of small cars, destroying property and leaving houses with their fronts cut off, like dollhouses. Yet still, life went forward. I could say the people were tough, but, really, what choice did they have but to carry on? More new thinking I wouldn't begin to apply to myself until later.

Just then, all I wanted was a shower. We checked into a small place in the village. The rooms were fifty dollars a night, and I know I used up my fifty in water. I simply stood there until my skin started to shrivel.

Next on the agenda was a beer, but the hotel didn't serve alcohol. We weren't that far into civilization. So the four of us set off down the dusty road in this typical, small African town, amid the bustle of people carrying their wares and folks on bikes tooting horns and church music pounding out from somewhere, until we found a decent bar that opened onto the road. One step closer to a sidewalk cafe than our lunch hanging over the river.

There we sat with our beers, chilling and reminiscing. The experience was still very much with us in our burning faces and hands, which made it that much easier to remember and talk about.

I wasn't keen on the food they were serving – fish – so I wandered further down the road, diary in hand, and found a man barbecuing chicken. I ordered some with vegetables, and he agreed to bring it to me back at the place where my friends were eating. Only in Africa. It all felt very minimalist. No excess there at the foot of the mountains.

It felt suddenly very beautiful, that life. A life that was an adventure, rather than merely a story. It was at that moment that the idea of writing this book glimmered faintly in my mind. But, clearly, I didn't race back to my room and begin hammering it out. There was still the trip back to Kenya ahead, which passed the next day almost in a blur. Breakfast, taxi, the flight to Entebbe, the airport in Nairobi. I don't even remember how we said goodbye. There was truly too much to say, too much to express. In truth, what we'd been through together didn't require words. It was felt, and that was enough.

I was suddenly in my car, driving through traffic to my flat, back to washing machines and Wi-Fi and clothing I hadn't been wearing for a week.

I wasn't ready for all that. As good as it was to be back in the land of modern conveniences, I needed space and time – and I needed for it to be outside. I couldn't initially cope with being indoors too much, as if I slowly needed to reintroduce myself to walls and ceilings. So I spent ages on my balcony, usually having a coffee and watching the world.

That was when I began to convert the experience I'd just survived into a new way of being. I had a new mind – one far different from the one that had pulled me through the hotel attack and the killing ascent to Margherita Peak. Now I had to determine how I was going to think and, more importantly, live, in that new way, as a new man.

I've done that in the year and some since I returned to Nairobi. I've done it in a way that I believe can work for other people as well. For anyone who wants to get past his or her fear and accomplish something personally significant.

And now I want to share that with you.

The start, at trekking services, Kilembe

Welcome to the Rwenzori national park

Local homes on the lower slopes.

The view from the base camp.

The summit!

The clouds parted just at the right moment.

Through the forest I took a moment to admire the beauty of the landscape.

The view towards Kilembe village and where our journey started.

Nearly back to the start, as we pass a local village school.

*Our post mountain chill out place was at a roadside restaurant
where the achievement really hit home.*

PART III
YOUR JOURNEY

EMBARKING

I DIDN'T SET ABOUT 2019 thinking I was going to write a book that year. I certainly never expected to be involved in the aftermath of a terrorist attack and definitely didn't think I would save a man's life nor get close to death myself. Sometimes the journeys just appear, and sometimes you just have to let them.

The journey I chose took me up one mountain with one mind. I came down with another. That new mind was the beginning of an entirely new way of living: a new way of taking journeys. I share that with you because we are all on journeys. Each day is a journey. Each day we have the opportunity to take a shot, to dissolve that nagging thought, to make that first step. But sometimes we simply become too fearful and we wait for another day. That day will forever be out of reach unless we start to do something about it.

The world is teeming with opportunities. They are yours for the taking. If you don't take one, that idea will keep floating around until someone else grabs it, leaving you to say, "I had that idea a few years ago." Anyone can have ideas, store them, forget them, but it's the doing something with them that's the hard part – and the part many avoid.

I learned from my mountain journey that to do something about the idea you have, you need to move through the stages of the prep, the journey, the setbacks and fears, the celebration at the summit, the downhill with the New You and the legacy you are creating. So now, let's look at where you are, where you want to be and how you're going to get there. Together we will again tackle the stages of a journey up your own mountain. As you're on your way, you'll be able to keep track and keep going, so that you don't have to hike back up this same path again. Yeah, it will occasionally be just like face-planting on a near-vertical snow field, but you'll keep moving in the right direction. Warning: just sitting there reading this will not be an option as we journey together.

This part of the book will take you on each section of the journey. It will give you things to think about, guide you in considering them and provide you with practical applications. You'll be able to take action on your journey, and the process will be embedded into a New You. Here's what that will look like in each of the chapters to follow:

- **Brief description of this part of your mountain journey**, a refresher, if you will, of the things I've introduced along the way in Part II.
- **The tools you'll need for each phase.** Only some of these will be physical ones. Most will be attitudes and the embracing of certain concepts.

- **The three big questions you'll need to have a think about for this part of the journey.** I'll provide examples to get you on the right track.
- **Actions to take.** These will be specific to you, though, again, I'll offer some samples to nudge you.
- **Last words on this part of the journey.** Just some thoughts to help you decide when you're ready for the next part of the journey.

Some basic 'rules' – which are actually more like guidelines – pieces of advice for you to take or leave. These guidelines apply to every part of the mountain journey and to every mountain you climb.

- *Love yourself.* You need to for any kind of mountain you face. Keep fit. Eat well. Hydrate. Maintain good posture. Keep your self-talk positive. The fact that you are reading this already makes you more self-aware than you have been in the past. Give yourself credit for that.
- *Be grateful.* That applies first of all to the small victories along the way. The small wins make you realize what you currently have going for you. If you didn't know you had some personal resources in place, you wouldn't be reading this book. If you've gotten this far, you believe in your ability to make progress. I do.
- *Have a vision and keep moving towards it.* Not just the overall objective of your particular journey (new job, better relationship, college degree), but all the

smaller goals along the way. Those are the ones that will keep you going.

- *Get support.* Let someone close to you know what you're doing so you can check in if progress gets tough – or you want somebody to celebrate with. A friend or family member may not be enough, though. You will need to surround yourself with like-minded or bigger-minded people who also want to grow. If you want to become great at something, you'll need to find the best person you can afford to help you be that. If you know getting fit and healthy is going to be a big challenge for you, start with your primary medical care provider. If fears and anxieties plague you, find a counsellor or a group. Sometimes employers have credible support systems. If not, feel free to start one to help yourself and others. Please do not see this book as a complete self-help guide to your overall mental health. We all need human beings on the journey.

- *Live as if you have already succeeded.* You were born a miracle, just like the most successful people on this planet. How you use your miracle brain, how you create and take advantage of opportunities – that's what makes the difference, and it starts with your belief in that. Wear the clothes you'll wear at the peak. Speak the language of those who are where you know you can be. Act like the person who deserves to reach this goal – because you do.

- *Have a routine.* If you're all over the place from first thing in the morning, you will probably struggle with remaining focused during the day. Start every day strong. Organize the morning. Create time and space to develop your vision, to formulate a plan and, later, as we'll see, to take steps toward your vision and to repeat the productive steps to create a habit. Get your end-of-day routine sorted too. It will settle the brain and help you sleep well. When it becomes necessary to tweak your routine, do it. In fact, refresh and update regularly.

- *Keep unnecessary distractions to a minimum.* That may mean turning off your cell phone while you're focusing on some part of your journey. It may involve limiting social media. Facebook and Twitter and all those venues are a part of life, but the frantic and erratic viewing of various online platforms to check for news information or how wonderful someone else's life is are just short-term, time-sapping mind distractions. Perhaps visits to Instagram or Snapchat or Facebook could take place only two or three times a day. Definitely avoid watching the news first thing when you wake up, and by all means don't watch right before bed. First thing in the morning and last thing at night are when your brain is most susceptible to suggestion, so this is the time to put *good* thoughts in there, not images of the latest murder or political debacle.

- *Breathe intentionally.* During the day, stop and breathe deeply, with focus. Breathe in through your nose, inflating all the way down to your belly and into your upper lungs. Count slowly as you ex-

181

hale, feeling your abdomen deflate into your spine. This action provides so much more oxygen to your body than your normal automatic breathing, and you will feel more awake and energized. The act of breathing in intention and breathing out tension creates freedom. Combine it with closing your eyes and feel the power of the breath run up your spine and into your brain. Follow it through. Even if you just do a few breaths hourly, that's great. If you are feeling like something is getting to you, take three deep breaths and feel the difference. Struggling? Just lie down and take note of how you breathe. You'll find yourself doing the above naturally.

- *Practise some form of meditation.* You don't have to become a yogi or a Zen master. I'm talking about a simple practice of getting still, taking several of those breaths we just talked about and then focusing on your normal breathing. If your thoughts wander, just gently bring them back to the breath. Feel it come in, hold and exhale. What you are practising is concentration. The meditation itself just happens; you can't 'make' it happen. Gradually, over time and with practice, those internal and external distractions will disappear. You may think nothing is going on that's beneficial, but you'll begin to notice, over time, that you are better able to focus during the day in a more relaxed way.

Just one final word before we embark. Taking a journey is about changing you, nobody else. All you can do is be transformed into an inspiration, a leader, someone who will set the pace so others follow. That is our final goal – to leave a legacy from each mountain we climb. Right now, though, let us begin where all journeys begin: with preparation.

CHAPTER FOURTEEN

THE PREPARATION

THE TRIP I MADE up the mountain took preparation, many years of it, to even have a go at that journey. Camping, running, hiking – it was all prep. And even after that, as you've seen in Part II, I still wasn't as ready as I thought I was. I learned, fortunately without serious physical injury, that preparing is so much better than trying to find a cure. A certain amount of thinking and getting-ready time needs to go into what *you* are about to embark upon as well, and that amount is usually far more than you think.

To use a more mundane example – since most of you won't be planning to climb the Rwenzori – once I was making a lemon drizzle cake. I had a vision of what the cake was supposed to be like: a beautifully warm dessert soaked in lemon-infused sugar syrup, just slightly crusty on the outside to give it a little crunch. I plunged right into the process. Boom boom boom, in go the ingredients. Whizz, mixed and into the tin. Straight in the oven. A little while later I'm checking it. It's changing colour, it's rising a little and it's smelling good – but it's taking longer than normal.

So, I skewer-check the cake. Odd. It's cooking on the outside and not the inside. Back in it goes, and the outside gets browner. Another check with a cooking skewer, but the middle is still soft. What's gone wrong? I had mixed the ingredients correctly, lined the tin, had it in the oven at the right ... ah ... that's when I noticed I was trying to oven-bake using the grill, which is never guaranteed to get the cooked-through result you're after. A momentary lapse in prep led to a grilled lemon drizzle something-like-a-cake. The outside that had been grilled was passable – though beyond 'slightly crusty' – but the inside was a sloppy, slightly warm mess. Basically inedible.

Prep requires focus all the way through. Rush the prep and you risk undoing any later good work. The more significant the journey you're about to take, the more thorough that preparation needs to be. A ruined lemon drizzle can be tossed in the bin with no real damage (except to your pride!). The climb toward a promotion, the formation of a new business, the healing of a wounded relationship – the rubbish bin is not the place you want those things to end up.

As you'll find in this chapter, just turning up does not constitute preparation, and it will not get you to the peak you want to reach. You may get along in your journey, but you may also collapse into a grilled lemon drizzle mess part way. You'll be wishing you'd spent that extra time up front.

Think of the prep phase of your journey as the foundation. If you've ever had a house built or watched a building under construction, you know that it seems to take forever to get that excavation and basement or slab done. You want to shout to those guys in their hard hats, "Seriously, can we get on with it?" But just as that concrete foundation will keep the structure from sinking into the ground like the Leaning Tower of Pisa, the foundation you lay for your own journey, if it's strong, can:

- Provide what you need to cope with any upcoming challenges that arise. And they will.
- Create flexibility in your mind. With a strong undergirding, you can look at more options to fit that frame.
- Keep you from having to constantly control. The foundation is there. No need to worry that someone else is going to come along and take it out. It's firm.
- Make you open to outside ideas. If they fit, you know where to place them. If they don't, thanks anyway.

Basically, if you skip or shorten the prep, you will embark on your life's dreams from an unstable start. Ask anyone who has married on a whim, or who is in fear the other person will change his or her mind before they get to the altar (A recipe for lasting happiness?). Or taken a course without the prerequisites (Lost, anyone?). Or told her boss she could take on a project without knowing what it entailed (Or maybe you crave high stress and poor results?). You get the idea.

If all of this puts you in panic mode and you want to return to couch-potato status, don't go there. In this chapter, we'll walk through the questions and challenges that tend to paralyze you if you don't confront them. Considering these questions one by one in the following pages will prevent you from setting yourself up to fail. If you'll remember from Chapter Six, I saw red flags in my preparation for the Rwenzori journey, and I ignored them or rationalized them away. What follows in this chapter is about helping you use the red flags and warning signs *you* see as points of preparation.

Tools for the Preparation Phase

Obviously, the specific tools you'll need for your particular journey will differ from those of someone who has a far different objective in mind. Courses to take, fitness goals to reach, list of people you'll need to help you – we'll get to all of that in Chapter Fifteen. Right now, let's look at the tools everyone needs to prepare for any kind of path.

Tool #1 A journal of some sort. This is not like keeping a daily diary, which many of us resolve to do on January 1 and have forgotten where we've mislaid it by January 15 – if we're disciplined enough to make it that long. The journal I'm recommending is any kind of notebook, blank book, sheets on a clipboard – a place where you can write, longhand. We're not talking something school-like. There are no wrong answers. No bad marks for spelling or penmanship (I personally write like a physician, without the medical degree as an excuse). As you are presented with questions in this chapter and the ones ahead, I urge you to write down your answers. The physical act of getting them on paper will drive you to where you want to be, or away from where you don't.

Tool #2 A willingness to be something different. This journey, if you choose the right one, will not only change your circumstances. It will change you. And probably for the better. You'll look at experiences differently. You'll drop some of the issues that have been dragging you down. You'll find yourself with more time to do the things you truly want to do. That sounds great, yes? But you'd be surprised how daunting it can seem to have a transformation of self, even if it means you'll be a stronger, wiser, more confident version of who you are now. Have a think about how willing you are to undergo significant change. As you think, write in that journal you're starting.

Tool #3 A metaphorical litter bin. Someplace to toss the handed-down, limiting ideas that have served you well up to now. It's one thing to crumple up the belief that you are too fat, too lazy, too shy, too obnoxious – whatever it is – and another to put it in a place where you can't dig it back up, smooth it out and embrace it again. That can be anything from the image of a rubbish bin to an actual wastepaper basket, the contents of which you burn whenever the litter starts accumulating. Whatever works for you – however you can toss out the things that hold you – it will allow you to rise to a level you thought was only for other people.

Tool #4 At least a modicum of belief in yourself. We all know or have heard about people who have raised families while working a full-time job and studying for a degree. Or those who've started over – successfully – after losing everything in a natural disaster or economic downturn. Or those who've walked away from the nine-to-five world to embrace their artistic yearnings. If one person can do it, surely any person can do it. If you disagree, now is a great time to write down WHY you can't get on board with that statement. Complete these sentences –

- *I can't do it because* _____
- *I may get started but I won't be able to finish because* _____
- *I might achieve this, but I'll probably be the same old me because* _____

Take another look at this list and include the things other people say that make you think you can't or won't. You're not a finisher. You've never done it before, so what makes you think you can do it now? Your destined trade is in your blood; what's with this whole college idea?

You can tear that page out of your journal, crumple it into a ball and toss it into your designated rubbish bin. Thank it for its assistance so far and then say, "Ciao! I won't be needing you any more." Or you can just visualize ripping it out and throwing it away at great speed, ejecting these limits from your mind. Feel different?

Those voices will try to pop up now and then, so be prepared for that. They like to chill out on the sofa and occasionally bark some orders, but that's just an opportunity for you to scoop them up and toss them. They won't really fight you. They want to hang out in the comfort of the place they know, and now and then they will try to make you do the same. But they won't try very hard. They're basically lazy. Thank them and tell them you've got stuff to do.

Speaking of stuff to do, if "... because I'm too busy" was one of your answers, write down everything you're busy doing. Then take a good, long, probing look at it. Are you busy with the right things? The things that will move you forward toward your vision? Or is your list dotted with social media, keeping a perfectly clean flat, partying so you won't feel left out, having a twice-weekly manicure. None of those things are bad in and of themselves, but do they fill up your days, leaving no room for anything of significance?

Bottom line: you have two options.

1. Option 1. You can talk to yourself and say you aren't good enough for this journey and never will be.

2. Option 2. You can talk to yourself and say you've got this. No problem. You're ready to give it your all.

Granted, they're just words, but those words have power. They feel different, because they are. If you choose Option 1, you are going to have a much harder time with the climb. Choose Option 2, and you are already preparing for success. That isn't all the preparation you'll need, but it's essential in order for the rest to do its job.

Take your time making sure those tools are at the ready. It may mean several days or even weeks of making your lists and tossing the limiting stuff and learning to talk more positively to yourself. At some point, you'll know you're ready to start the specific preparation for your own journey. How will you know?

- You'll find yourself restless to get started
- You'll flip ahead in this book
- You'll be able to look at yourself in the mirror and say, "I can at least prepare, right?"

When you reach that place, you're ready to move on to some important personal questions.

The Three Questions for Preparation

Question 1. Where are you in your life right now?

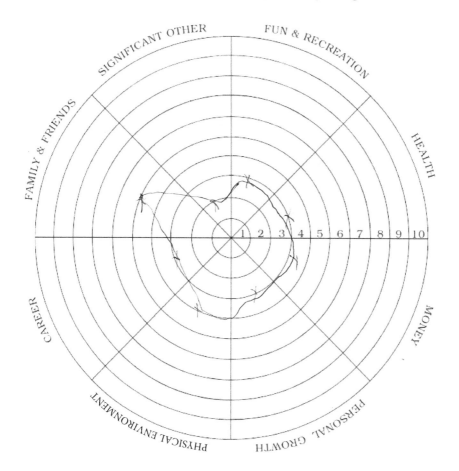

How *do* you know where you are? How can you determine where you're going currently? One way is to work with the Wheel of Life. I didn't invent this. The original Wheel of Life is attributed to Paul J. Meyer, a thought leader from the 60s, but has been used and modified many times. I've found it to be an extremely helpful tool in discovering exactly where I stand.

Here's how I suggest you use it:

1. We'll start with something separate from the wheel itself. Begin by listing your personal values. What are the things that are most important to you? Write them down in order, so that number one is the golden thread through all the others. If you struggle with an order, that's fine. Just write them down. You can reorganize them later. Understanding your values is key to knowing your inner self. If you're thinking, "Um, what's a value?" look at it as an inner principle that you hold true. It's something you can't give up – something you'd fight for. No matter what happens to you, you stick by it. If someone disputes it, that hits a nerve in you.

Examples:
- Integrity
- Self-respect
- Respect for others
- Generosity
- Courage

These are the lenses through which you look at life. Be honest, and if security, financial success and fame are your values, write them down. Don't try to make the list look good, because, (a) no one but you is going to see it and, (b) if you lie to yourself, you're already shooting yourself in the foot.

Put this list aside.

CHAPTER FOURTEEN: THE PREPARATION

2. Back to the wheel. The areas on the wheel represent various aspects of a person's life. If you want to change any of them to fit your own personal circumstances, feel free. After all, it's your wheel and your life. For instance, you may want to include Spiritual or, if you're retired, to replace Work with Volunteering.

3. Have a think about each segment. Zero is where you would be least satisfied. Ten is top of the pops and where you are most satisfied. Have a look at each segment and score it by marking each across the line at the level where you honestly find yourself right now.

4. When you connect the marks across all segments, you've made your wheel. It's probably going to be pretty wonky-looking because most of us don't have balanced lives until we become intentional.

5. Now look at your list of values and see how that matches up with the wheel you've just created. If you listed Work as your number one value, is it one of those on the wheel that you're most satisfied with? How about Fun, Time, etc.?

The first time I did this I was over 40 years old. I had never been asked to grade elements of my life, or even to list my personal values. That meant I'd spent four decades living blind. Once I did my scoring, I had a 7 here, a 3 there, a 5 over there. When I connected them … there was no way that wheel was turning. I'd been on a bumpy ride all my life.

Probably more importantly, the wheel was not a reflection of the values I'd written down. I had high scores on the wheel for Fun and Adventure but scored low on Relationships. That conflicted with the fact that Relationships was at the top of my values list. And that was just the start. There I was with my bumpy, less-than-perfect wheel and thinking, "I'm a mess. What now?"

The wheel is an indication of where you're out of balance and where your priorities conflict with your values. Our goal is to get that wheel as close to round as possible. When it's round, life is going to run far more smoothly.

Working with the wheel helped me prepare for the right journeys. I saw that I needed to work out my less-than-satisfactory finances – a worthwhile journey. I recognized that my relationships were not great and I needed to remedy that – another significant climb. Probably my most valuable realization was that I didn't have time to do much other than run on a treadmill of life, but ironically my physical fitness was not where I wanted it to be.

With your journal in front of you, write what comes to you as you think about these questions:

- How do I feel about my scores? Initial reaction. (Don't overthink this one or judge yourself. It is what it is right now.)
- Looking at the higher scores, how much time am I devoting to those? Is it time well spent, or is it costing me in other important areas?
- What would a 10 look like in the low-scoring areas? What would I be doing if that 3 were a 10?

- Do I have space in my life to make the improvements needed for my wheel to turn smoothly? What might I have to give up? Am I *ready* to give those things up?
- What is stopping me from making any area that isn't a 10 into a 10? Remember that we're talking about *satisfaction* here. If you're truly content with not bringing in 7 or even 6 figures a year, fabulous. Give yourself a 10 for Money. This is about honest satisfaction, according to *your* true values.

What do the answers to these questions provide for you? They hopefully give you a clear picture of where you are so that, as we move forward with Questions 2 and 3, you'll discover what you need to do in to prepare for a journey you've longed to take, a journey we'll define with more clarity in Chapter Fifteen. For now, perhaps you know:

- What you truly value most
- What you may have to change in your life to live congruently with those values
- What you're already doing to live well ... which leads us to our next question

Question 2. What do you already have going for you that could benefit you on this journey you long to take?

Sometimes finding out that your Wheel of Life is decidedly lopsided can make you feel like complete rubbish. That is not the intention, trust me. You are here, reading this book and hopefully thinking and writing and using it to take you forward. The simple fact you *want* to take a journey toward a better life and a better self speaks well of you. Remember, you are not failing if you have a lopsided wheel. It's those who are doing *nothing* about their situation who are letting themselves down. It's important to take stock of what you already have going for you as you prepare for this new phase. And that involves discovering what it is that provides your moral direction – what makes you get up and do.

We're talking about your *internal moral compass,* the strengths that have allowed you to be successful in the past, that have brought you to this good place where you want to go further and higher and deeper. And do better.

Try this:

1. Make a list of all the things you have achieved, accomplished, mastered or simply done well in your adult life. These can include anything from travel to getting a certified qualification to finishing reading a book. From being loyal to the company you work for to learning to drive even though you were terrified. From getting a licence to practise massage or style hair or teach yoga to taking care of a sick parent or saving a wounded marriage or mastering a souffle. Write until you can't think of any more. Come back to your list later and add more.

2. Deeply ponder that list and then make a new one, writing down the strengths, the qualities it took to bring those things to fruition. You will probably find yourself writing down some of the same traits

over and over. I'm referring to things like *loyalty, the ability to see the big picture, plain stubbornness, compassion, uncanny intuition, an analytical mind, good manners.* The possibilities are vast. Don't discount anything as being common to everybody, because most good qualities aren't.

These are some of the same traits that will enable you to make this next journey. Obviously, you'll need to discover additional ones or hone the ones inherent in you. But this list shows that you already have a great deal in your favour that makes success a more viable possibility.

I carry my list with me and I make sure, every day, I'm living by these strengths, which in essence correlate to my values (More on this later when we talk about your Creed). This is continuing preparation for what comes next.

Question 3. *Where are you NOT helping yourself move forward?*

Just as it's important to know your strengths as you prepare for the climb, it's essential to be aware of your challenges as well. You know what I mean: the limitations that always seem to hold you back from ever reaching for what you want.

Think of this as a *fixed mindset* that causes you to plateau and achieve less than you're capable of. What might a boss say about you on an evaluation?

- Avoids challenges?
- Gets defensive when criticized?

- Gives up easily?
- Sees effort as fruitless?
- Ignores feedback?
- Feels threatened by the success of others?

If the boss image doesn't work for you, think of a good, critical friend, your spouse who is likely to be pretty honest or a university professor writing you a reference to a prospective employer. You may have another scenario. Use whatever works for you.

Let's go back to your journal and do the same process we used to recognize your strengths.

1. Write down all the situations in your adult life in which you feel like you failed or, at the very least, fell short. Don't beat yourself up. Just observe your past. If you feel like this might be an endless list, choose only six things.

2. Being as honest with yourself as you can, write down the habits that contributed to those disappointing outcomes. Avoid placing blame on other people involved, even if they were actually complicit. We're just focusing on *your* share of the responsibility right now. Again, you may find that your answers are consistent across several circumstances.

It isn't a bad idea to keep a list of those tendencies with you as well. You may think of this as a downer, but believe me, seeing weaknesses comes in very handy when a relationship or task isn't going well. You can check the list to see if any of your old mindset is contributing to this thing heading south.

Notice that I've said *old* mindset. That's because right now we're going to reframe that into a *growth mindset*. You know what your challenges are now. A vital part of your preparation is to learn the opposite of what is currently holding you back.

- Embraces challenge!
- Persists in the face of setbacks!
- Sees effort as the path to being the best self possible!
- Learns from criticism by thinking of it as feedback!
- Finds lessons in the successes of others and is inspired by them!

Sounds great, but is it possible? I can only assure you that it is by telling you more of my own story.

For years I lived a life where I believed I was doing well. I had a good job, and I was relatively successful at it. I had a house. I could take a holiday once a year.

But if I received any negative feedback, I automatically registered that as 'their' error, not mine. Clearly 'they' hadn't listened to me.

I always did what *I* knew to be best and continued to do that. Until it got too difficult. Then I always found a way to give up.

After a while, I began to wonder why things just kept going wrong. How was it that I could never get my point of view across? Why weren't people listening to me? It finally occurred to me that what I was doing was the very definition of insanity: doing the same thing the same way and expecting different results.

By then I was working across cultures and with many different people from diverse backgrounds. I made a conscious effort to pick up on the various ways they approached things. Some believed that it was down to others to help them, understand them, see it their way. Others, however, seemed to take control of their own inner moral compass and stay on a steady track. No one was coming to enable them. It was down to *them*.

What would happen if I did the same? If I took charge of my destiny? I knew what would happen if I didn't. I would continue to live in the cycle of half-hearted effort, disappointment and blame.

I started small. I wrote out my limiting mindset and the growth mindset and stuck them up on my wall. Every morning when I woke up, I read the items on the growth mindset. There was no point in reading the limiting mindset. I already had that one down, and I didn't need to be reminded. I wanted to understand what it would take to be better.

I picked one line from the growth mindset – which was to listen more to other people's thoughts and opinions – and made it my day's mission to focus on that. After practising that for no more than a few days, I started to realize that I did not have the monopoly on good ideas. A lot of people around me had excellent thoughts, and many of them could make mine even better. They could personally and emotionally help me. Got it cracked!

I moved to the next growth set item, which was to learn from those who disagreed with me. They also served a purpose. I could recoil and stay with the same limiting mindset, refusing to even consider another point of view, going back to item 1. After all, leaving the comfort zone is always a scary proposition. But I couldn't forget that first item I had mastered, so instead I put the second to work. I could be open and learn and be inspired. As often as possible, I chose the second approach, but I didn't forget the first – I just built on it.

Eventually I was doing that day's best at all the items on my list. Now, let's be real: some days I had lapses (and so will you). All of that was hugely difficult for my personality: a go-getting, proactive and sometimes impatient one. With criticism and judging others the norm in my family of origin, it's not surprising I grew up defensive, argumentative and judgemental. I had no idea to learn how to reframe that, so it took, and sometimes continues to take, a great deal of effort. But one day of a limiting mindset is better than *every* day in that mindset, which is where I was before I began. Just remember, as I had to, that this changing of mindset is not a one-off. Get ready for continual work. This is not just your preparation. It's your ongoing challenge.

Action

So far, all the preparation we've thought about is internal. By now you're probably ready to put this to use in a concrete way. We'll do that by using all the inner work you've just done.

In your journal – or in a larger format so you can look at the big picture – whichever works for you:

1. Write down the three areas on your Wheel of Life where you would like to be more satisfied.
2. Under each one, list five actions you can take to improve in each of those three areas. Five. It must be five. If you struggle to come up with five, keep thinking. You'll get there. The first three may come easily, and the fourth and fifth will probably require some depth. It is likely that is where the real impact can be achieved.

It will look like this:

First Area Where I'd Like to Be More Satisfied

1. _FAMILY_
2. _HEALTH_
3. _MONEY_
4. _CAREER_
5. _FUN + RECREATION_

Second Area Where I'd Like to Feel More Satisfied

1. _____
2. _____
3. _____
4. _____
5. _____

Third Area Where I'd Like to Feel More Satisfied

1. _____
2. _____

3. _____

4. _____

5. _____

3. Now, from each list of five, pick three that will transform your life. Not the easiest ones to do, but those that will provide a challenge, that will test you in a way that ultimately improves you and, eventually, other people. Choose the ones to which your first reaction is, "I can't do that!"

4. Commit to doing the three things you've selected in each of those three areas. This is like training for a marathon. You wouldn't set out to run 26.2 miles without some pretty intense prep. Yes, this is focused and intense and challenging. Without it, you're not going to get there. I guarantee it.

5. Most people can't do this all at once. Take the first item on your list and give it a go for a week. Maybe this week you'll focus on hearing other people's opinions and really understanding what they say and how they say it. You'll listen with empathy, trying to see what their map of the world looks like. When you feel like you're beginning to master that, go to your next item. If you *are* capable of taking on more than one at a go, do it. Just take the time to master. If something takes more than a week to sink in, that's okay.

6. Layer week two onto week one and so on. The effect will be cumulative. Soon enough you'll notice a difference in the amount of information, additional

knowledge and understanding of other people you have. You'll even be able to pick up on other people's language and think, "Aha! You have a limiting mindset." Just don't point it out to them.

7. It helps me to keep those in the back of my journal. No point in trying to keep nine goals in your head. Have them there, like a creed, and take them with you wherever you go. Let's see what happens along the way.

Time to Move On to the Next Phase?

Hopefully you're excited and keen to get on the road. Keep that enthusiasm, but don't let it keep you from this key part of the journey, no matter what you're embarking on. How *do* you know when your internal preparation is complete and you're ready to go forward?

First of all, be careful about your expectations. Your current mindset has been ingrained in you over time, and the longer it has been in operation the longer it will take for the new growth mindset to take hold. You don't have to wait until you feel no resistance at all to criticism and feedback, or until your field of vision is as wide as the sky. But give yourself time for these changes to begin to become a natural part of the way you are in the world.

Keep in mind that the inner work you're doing *is* moving you forward. It isn't pre-journey stuff. It is the start of the journey itself. This is the beginning of the path. There are no wings to carry you over this to the end.

If you need something more concrete, here are some signs that you're prepared enough to move into the next phase:

- When you hear the doubting inner voices, you can easily say, "Yeah, thanks, but I'm good"
- You've gotten rid of the busywork in your life
- You can look in the mirror and say – out loud – "I have SO got this" and believe it
- You can see how your Wheel of Life is about to get rounder. You're confident of that.
- You can read through your limiting mindset and say, "That's totally not me any more"
- You can read through the growth mindset and say, "Holy smokes, I'm getting there!"
- You can see measurable progress in your nine areas. Maybe you're noticing less resistance to feedback or you're listening where you used to insist on having the floor or you've taken on a new challenge without telling yourself you'll probably quit halfway through.

You may go ahead with your journey and realize there's something you need to do before you can take the next step. You realize your confidence needs a boost or you remember someone who's been there who just might have some good advice for you. It isn't backsliding to need to stop and prep some more and then go on. It's being smart.

For now, though, if you can feel it in your own progress, your own compass, that it's time to start the next chapter, do it. Let's get in there and vividly define your journey and clarify what you'll need in order to take it.

CHAPTER FIFTEEN

DEFINING YOUR JOURNEY

BECAUSE I WAS RELATIVELY FIT in January 2019, I could have climbed a number of different mountains in Africa. I chose Margherita Peak on Mount Stanley in the Rwenzori, and I wish I could say that was because it was the highest peak in Uganda and I wanted to challenge myself physically, emotionally, spiritually – whatever. But that wouldn't be entirely honest. Okay, it wouldn't be honest at all.

I sort of found myself on that journey because Jake, who I'd climbed Mount Kenya with in 2018, suggested we do a mountain a year. I said I was in. There were few things I liked better than a hike, so why not? That was the extent of my choosing process.

As you know, it turned out to be a great deal more than a hiking expedition.

Now when I set out to do something important in my life, I'm far more mindful of exactly what it is I'm embarking on and why. Having done the inner prep, and continuing to do that on a daily basis, I can focus on defining each journey. That's what we'll focus on together in this chapter. Whether you're thinking of starting something new, reshaping something you're already involved in or leaving behind something old and unhealthy, you'll need to be able to envision what's before you, in detail, as far as you can at this point. You'll have to name it. Map it out. And foresee the possible obstacles that could try to defeat you along the way.

Let's look at this concept of potential roadblocks for a moment. We'll examine the specific barricades that could be thrown up in your way a little later, but for now, think about what such an impediment means – because it *will* be there, no matter what path you take.

You know what it's like to be travelling and you see that dreaded sign that says *ROAD CLOSED.* You get your hackles up. You've got somewhere to be and a certain time to be there. Why is the universe conspiring against you? The fist comes down on the steering wheel. You lean on the horn – as if *that* is going to move you one inch further along – and you may even get out of the vehicle with your binoculars to peer ahead to see just what the – insert your go-to profanity – the hold-up is.

Eventually, of course, someone will come along and reroute you, or the road will reopen. Never in the history of car trips has a road just simply been closed forever and the drivers left to figure out a way to get on with it. And at some point, you discover what caused the way to be blocked. A gigantic tree fell across it. A heavy rain brought down a landslide of mud that obliterated the highway. A ten-car pile-up has occurred, with fatalities. The universe has not conspired against you after all. It has instead sent in the ultimate kinetic action to get your attention and tell you it's dangerous to go on in this direction at this time.

But do you give up the journey completely? Probably not, unless you were involved in that accident or were hit by that tree or caught in that mudslide – which would be an entirely different scenario. We're talking about the blocks that slow you down, make you pause until you can figure out a way around that obstacle – a way to alter your route without abandoning the trek altogether.

Being able to predict some of those hindrances is an important part of defining and mapping out your journey. Again, we'll discuss this in more detail later in the chapter. I bring up the concept now so that before you even have a chance to start second-guessing this new thing you want to undertake for your life you'll know that, just because there are speed bumps, that doesn't mean you have to give up before you even begin.

If you'll remember, in Chapter Seven I talked about some people being like a river, which flows and meanders as it continues on its way. Others tend to be more like a reservoir, resigning themselves to "it can't be done" and sticking with their current lot in life. Hopefully, after your focus in Chapter Fourteen, you realize you *are* a river, be it the ancient Thames, the creature-ridden Amazon or the mighty Mississippi. You are your own unique body of moving water, no longer content to remain as you are and perhaps go stagnant. Knowing that about yourself, you are ready to determine just what this amazing journey of yours will be.

Tools for Defining the Journey

As we've said already, every journey will be different, so the specific tools for your particular journey will vary as well. There are, however, certain inner qualities you need to have in your kit to define this path you want to take.

*Tool #1. A willingness to **be** different than you are right now.* This carefully mapped-out journey you are about to take may change your circumstances. You might end up with a promotion or a different job completely – maybe even a whole new career. Perhaps you'll enjoy a fresh relationship or be more stimulated by the one you're in. Depending on what you're choosing to do, you could look different, be more fit, have new skills, or live in a new place. Fabulous.

However, no matter what physical and situational changes take place, you are also going to be a changed person within. The person you are now will not be the same one who becomes the regional manager or writes the novel or moves to Switzerland. You're going to be more confident and less concerned about pleasing everybody. You'll have become strong and clear-eyed and not concerned about what people think of you. You won't let obstacles (or people) intimidate you, and you *will* do what is yours to do despite the flak you may receive.

Before you say, "Well, yeah, I'm willing to change that way. Who *wouldn't*?"

Who wouldn't?

- Someone who will have to hear, "You're not as 'nice' as you used to be." (Translation: "You aren't a doormat any more and that isn't working for me.")
- Someone who will have to deal with, "I think you're selfish. Crazy. Too old." Take your pick. (Translation: "You are going outside the box and that scares the hell out of me. Stop it.")
- Someone who will no doubt be treated to, "This is ridiculous. You've never acted this way before. No!" (Translation: "This means I have to shift too. And I don't want to.")

Being different from the way you are in the world now is going to make you feel great – and possibly make other people feel like their underwear is giving them a rash. Arm yourself now. Be more willing to be different than you are willing to stay comfortable.

*Tool #2. A willingness to **do** different.* It's pretty obvious that if you're on a journey to change something in your life you're going to do that thing in a new way. Just be aware that this 'differentness' will spill over into the way you do just about everything.

If you're changing the way you are in relationship with your significant other, you'll change the way you are in all your relationships. It will simply happen.

If you're taking a new approach to bettering your position in the workplace, you'll take that approach in your fitness programme and your volunteer work as well.

How you do something is how you do everything. So be more willing to do life differently than you are to stay right where you are.

Tool #3. A willingness to respond to the naysayers. This is something like Tool #1, except that it isn't a matter of simply moving forward despite the comments and the cautions and even the ridicule. Some people aren't just going to shake their heads and walk away. Parents, spouses, close friends, pastors, your kids – those folks will persist, and they can't be ignored. In some cases, they have a right to an explanation for why you have done a one-eighty and are not quite the same person you were even a week ago.

Your immediate family may be concerned for your safety – mentally, emotionally and physically.

Your counsellor or spiritual advisor might think you're getting dangerously far from the accepted norms and conventions.

Your friends could conceivably fear that you're going to leave them behind.

Your employer can doubt your loyalty to the organization.

These well-meaning people in your life want you to walk up the mountain with a bungee cord wrapped round your waist so they can pull you back down to their accustomed place. Are you willing to produce your scissors and cut that bungee? Or better yet, are you willing to snap the thing and catapult on up the hill? The freedom sounds great, but it comes at a cost. Count it first before you begin to map your journey.

And here's how to do that.

Make sure that this thing you want to do, accomplish, achieve or change is the right journey for *you*. Consider these questions in your journal:

- Is this desire *your* desire? Or is it something someone else thinks you should do? Or something that is simply 'done' in the family or community or culture you've grown up in? Everybody becomes a teacher in the Jones clan. Everyone in the upper middle class gets a university education. Most people from your town stay there. If that isn't what *you* want, you'll struggle to answer the people who question your choice.

- Do you really *need* to make this journey? You might be guaranteed a higher salary if you get a master's degree, but will it make you a happier, more satisfied person? You could very well get to the place where you can lift more than anyone else in the gym, and yet will that take you anyplace you want to go? If not, you've got nothin' for those people who try to change your mind.

- Would you much rather be on a *different* journey? Do you read or hear about happy, flourishing people and long to do what they're doing? While you're planning to move up to the next level in your career, do you actually want to develop your musical talent instead? Even as you set out to become a graphic designer, would you prefer to be discovering yourself as a painter? As you are making a plan to become a nurse, do you truly want to do medical research instead? If you have no passion for this thing you're setting out to do, you'll believe anybody who tells you where you ought to be going.

Whatever the journey you have in mind as you move into this phase, be sure it is:

- The one you want to be on.
- The one that allows you to say, "thanks for sharing" to the naysayers and go forward with it anyway
- The one that is really going to change things for you
- The one you can't wait to wake up for every day, no matter how many obstacles drop in your way

Let's see what that looks like as you define where you're going.

The Three Questions for Defining Your Journey

Question #1. What is the TRUE journey you want to take?

Right now, in your journal, write down your can't-wait-to-get-started journey as you see it now. Just a simple statement. *I want to walk the El Camino in Spain. I want to run the Boston Marathon. I want to write an epic romance. I want to have joint custody of my children. I want to establish a vegetable garden that will feed my family. I want to lose fifty pounds. I want to quit smoking.*

When you've written that statement in bold in your journal, ask yourself these questions and write your answers:

How is this journey important for me?

Why is it important to me?

Is it a journey I can take even if people tell me I'm nuts?

Is this journey going to change things for me in a positive way?

Do I have a passion for this journey?

Tweak as necessary until you have complete, honest answers.

If you're still having trouble defining it, go back to your Wheel of Life and your values as you worked with them in Chapter Fourteen. Consider – preferably as you journal – the following:

- The areas on your wheel where you're currently not as satisfied as you'd like to be. Want more adventure? Then deciding to take a week to follow Hadrian's Wall is a great choice. Reading *War and Peace* – not so much (unless nothing says adventure to you like a little Tolstoy). Want more satisfaction in the spiritual realm? Planning a retreat makes perfect sense. Becoming a licensed accountant does not.

- The values on your list that aren't congruent with the wheel. Family is #1 but you're not satisfied in that area? Then maybe go with instituting some family traditions rather than setting your sights on becoming a master golfer right now. Security is #1 but your money area is practically microscopic on the wheel? You'll probably want to opt for getting a promotion instead of planning a trip to the Virgin Islands.

- Think about what you really stand for. Be it social justice, world peace, historic conservation or saving the environment, why not choose a journey that will help you make a difference in that cause?
- Without any "Yeah, buts", think about the things that create flow in your life, even for short periods. Consider what motivates you. What makes you daydream. Those are your indicators that a journey needs to be taken so that you can have more of that flow. More of that energy. More of that passion.

It is so hammered into us to make money, get approval and stay secure that considerations like these can seem unrealistic. If that's the case for you, try this approach.

Imagine you have passed away. (You don't have to go into a lot of detail here. It doesn't matter whether you had an accident, were murdered or suddenly had an aneurism. The point is, you're gone.) You've left a grieving family and friends as well as a lot of unfinished business, and it's funeral time.

Someone is going to get up and give a eulogy or at least some remarks about you and your life. He or she will hastily create something because you've unexpectedly left everyone with things to sort out. It comes out kind of generic. *She was a good woman. He was a family guy.* Something that could be said about ninety per cent of the population.

Now, rewind. You know you're going to die. Happens to the best – and the worst – of us. You have the opportunity to influence what that person is going to say to all those who gather to say goodbye, cry, laugh and probably drink and eat food at your expense. Surely it's only right that the person who is given that job can describe you and your achievements as you wish, yes?

What do you want that person to say? Write your own eulogy. I've done it and found the result to be profound. It talks about the wrong paths I took, my bumpy journey. But as I was writing it, it got me thinking about the right paths, the smooth roads I would want my eulogizer to be able to truthfully speak of. How could I make them real? It went beyond, "Wouldn't it be nice to help some orphans?" to "I am going to find out how I can do that – and then do it."

I'm not going to lie: it was an emotional experience. But it forced me to get on with life in a more productive way. It made me do what I wanted to do. Scary? Yes. And yet it led me to creating two businesses – not just thinking about it, but doing it. I completed a university course, having previously failed at my college education. I became a qualified posture therapist and, of course, wrote this book.

This exercise goes far deeper than a bucket list. This is about your deepest desires, your best ideas. It's about the person you want to be.

Now fast forward. Choose one of those things you want said about you at your final celebration of life. Make it your next journey.

Write it down in your journal. It may be different from the statement you made at the beginning of our discussion of Question #1. Hopefully it will be clearer, more sharply defined.

And yet there's more …

Question #2. How will you know you have achieved it?

You've read that right. Before you map out how to get there, you have to know what 'there' is. You need a vision of exactly what it's going to look like when you reach completion. You need to be able to visualize the finish line of this successful journey. In essence, you're starting at the end as you take these steps.

1. Find a place and a block of time where you can be alone and undistracted. Close your eyes and just imagine exactly what it will look like to have completed this journey you've chosen. See it. Hear it. Smell it. Touch it. Taste it. Experience it within.

2. Take up your journal again. Complete this sentence by filling in the blanks below. *When I have reached the end of this journey:*
   I will be _____
   I will have _____

I will feel _____

I will know _____

3. Under each one, write a paragraph in as much detail as you can. Get it down to the clothes you'll be wearing, the conversations you'll be having, the way your body will be feeling.

Sound too woo-woo for you? Too silly? Too childish? Actually, this kind of dreaming is innate in us as human beings. Kids do it all the time, not because they're immature, but because no one has told this them yet: *Sure, that's all very nice, but this is the real world. Time to study, get a job, settle down and, for God's sake, be normal.*

The truth is, the finest inventions, advancements and progressive ideas have all started in someone's imagination, and that someone was an adult. Children dream of fairy-tale weddings, unicorns, chocolate, Peter Rabbit or themselves as heroes. Adults, if they allow themselves to, envision lives that can far exceed what they're experiencing now.

I have a friend who is employed in what to many would seem to be a great job. When I asked him what his dream is, I half-expected him to say, "I'm living it!" Instead, he surprised me with this.

"I would love to be an archaeologist. I would love to be digging up Roman ruins, seeking to understand what and how it all happened."

As he spoke, I could see his body uplift. His voice changed, gained energy. The passion showed on his face, and he was more animated with his gestures. It was clear that he could see himself doing it, even though his current life involved nothing remotely archaeological. We found his way of living in the future.

I can hear some of you saying, "You can't live in the future!" (i.e. "You can't dream! It's pointless!")

Let's turn that around for a minute. Can you recall a moment in your past? Good or bad, can you imagine it? I'm sure you can, and as you do, you probably feel much the same way you did then. Maybe your heart beats faster or you get that anxious churning in your stomach, or you grin lobe to lobe. That's because, as brain researchers have discovered in studying people with post-traumatic stress, the activity in the brain when someone is in the midst of an actual crisis and when that person remembers the crisis is exactly the same. In both cases the brain activates the stress or the feel-good hormones – cortisol or serotonin, for example – and the body reacts.

It is the same thing when you imagine the future. As you envision it in detail, your heart may race, your energy rise, your thoughts become more positive. The very act of dreaming tells your brain it's happening, which gets those endorphins going and suddenly you can feel yourself at the end of that journey. And it rocks.

So, yeah, make those dreams big. Vivid. Full of all the emotions of a positive event. See your journey like it's happening. Better yet, see it and feel it as if it has *already* happened. Simply by doing that you have started moving toward making it so.

Do it. If you really want it, then believe it and dream it in detail. Write it down, adding specifics to what you've already penned or typed.

This is your journey. Now, how are you going to get there?

Question #3. Continuing to work backwards, what might the journey itself look like?

You know where you want to end up. And you want the old saying to be true, that getting there is half the fun. What's it going to take for both the journey and the destination to fit your dream? What does the map look like?

That can seem overwhelming, but I use a method created by Brian Mayne that I hope will be helpful to you. You might know it by a different name, but I call it a flip chart.

A flip chart is an oversized piece of paper about the size of a forty-inch television, routinely seen at those annoying workshops where you are split into groups to do a group task. It's the place where thoughts are collected from the group by the scribe, to be awkwardly presented to the class.

But we are going to use it to map out our dreams, Nothing annoying or awkward involved.

Action

First, tear a sheet from the rest of the pad. Find yourself a decent marker or pen in whatever colour you like or even many colours – it doesn't matter. You'll need a way of sticking this to the wall or another vertical surface such as an easel so that it's prominently displayed for you to see it every day. Plan where you'll hang it, but don't do that yet.

Lay the sheet out on a horizontal surface and write your journey – your goal, your vision – in big, bold letters at the top. This is the specific achievement you want to complete, as you've defined it in this chapter.

Next, move to the bottom of the page and draw a massive arrow from there towards your goal at the top.

On the left, write down all the small steps you need to take to make that vision happen. You may not capture everything in one go, and that's fine. You can add to this as you think of and discover all the things you need to do. You'll be grateful for this list as, when you achieve each one, you can tick it off. That's very satisfying and shows you that you're making progress.

On the right side, you have a space for drawing. Most of us are not artists, so if you are anything like me the drawings will only mean something to you and be unrecognizable without explanation to others. Again, that's fine. This is for your eyes only. The benefit is in the doing. Sketching draws on the creative, right side of your brain, which is as important to mapping as the analytical, left side.

The drawings are designed to be progressive. So, starting where you are, draw you taking the step that mirrors the activity on the left. See the steps visually and increasing in size as you get closer to realizing your vision.

This is your map which can be added to, drawn on and tweaked. Do I actually use these charts? Yep. My corridor at home has flip charts stuck up, the objective at the top of each one, the massive arrow, the steps, the drawings. They aren't artistic or even neat, but they work for me.

There is something about walking past those flip charts, stopping and having a read. Not only do you see what you have to do – you find yourself doing it. I ticked each one off and, seemingly all of a sudden, I had a business. It didn't stop there as, once the business was up and running, it was about refining, for which I used the same process. It is this process that helped me take the first steps to writing this book. I jotted down ideas on the flip charts, I tried things out as I read and educated myself. I had started, and from there I held myself accountable to my chart, my map.

Time to Move On to the Next Phase?

No plan is set in stone. Flexibility and a willingness to reroute when necessary are key as you move ahead. Before you take that first step, though, ask yourself these things. Hopefully you'll write your answers in your journal:

- Am I absolutely clear on where I want to go and how I'll know when I get there?
- Do I feel confident enough in the wisdom of this journey to simply thank the naysayers for their input and move forward anyway?
- Is my flip chart clear and organized and detailed enough that any time I look at it I understand how I'm going to get where I'm headed?

- Does the thought of starting to do all the things on the chart get me out of bed in the morning with a purpose? (Beyond getting my hands on a cup of coffee?)

If you have to answer no to any of those questions, that just means you're being honest. You only need a little more clarity or confidence or organization or passion. So go back to those places in this chapter and do a little more dreaming. A little more journaling. A little more planning.

No one sets out with complete assuredness, but that's part of the adventure. If you're feeling a little trepidation, yet you can't imagine *not* taking this journey, you're ready for the next phase. Let's go for it.

CHAPTER SIXTEEN

FACING THE FEARS

I HOPE, AS YOU MAPPED OUT your journey to a new place and a New You in Chapter Fifteen, you felt the deep joy that comes with new opportunity. By now maybe you've taken those first few steps and have experienced that confidence which only comes with knowing where you want to go and moving toward it with a plan.

And then ... boom.

Whether it's happened to you yet or not, trust me, it will: an old fear suddenly pops to the surface and you recoil back into your comfort zone. Before you even realize it, you are reacting the way you always have. *I was stupid to even start this. What was I thinking? I can't do this – and if I do, what if ...?*

When that happens – not *if* it happens – you can be assured that you're perfectly normal. It's part of the way we're nurtured. In the first years of our lives, most of us are taught by those closest to us – usually our parents – to adopt certain limiting beliefs. That's basically done in the interest of protecting us, which isn't necessarily a bad thing, but it can be. Let me give you an example.

One traditional UK summer afternoon (i.e. windy and wet) when I was very young – not more than a carefree five years old – my dad and I were playing football with an oversized beach ball on a beautiful patch of grass which happened to be at a clifftop. You see where this is going, right? As the ball rolled between us, the wind caught it and blew it toward said cliff. My mission was to save that ball from rolling over the side, so I ran for it. While in mid-dive in its direction, I could hear the frantic shouting from behind me. Obviously, since I'm here to tell you the story, I did not topple over the edge. Instead, it was game over, and I was marched back to the house for being, well, a kid, basically.

You may very well say, *Of course you needed to be taught about what's dangerous!* and as a father I completely agree. However, it's the *way* an understanding of peril is shared that makes the difference.

I was 'told' (translation: lectured by an irate father) what it looks like from that precipice and what happens when you fall from it. In grim detail. I was given an intense tutorial on how I could have died – in even grimmer detail. And maybe worst of all, it was decreed there would be no more football with Dad on that perfect grassy spot. So no opportunity to learn caution.

From my point of view, I had saved the ball and I *hadn't* fallen over, so what was the crisis? Yet from that day on, I was left with a fear of heights that took me years to get over. Obviously I did, or you wouldn't have caught me even close to the Rwenzori or any other mountain range. But it took until after my own children were grown up to recover, so no doubt my fear rubbed off on them. Or maybe I rubbed it *in* with all my cautions about edges and falling and death.

Did my dad do the wrong thing? Not in terms of the basic message that you have to be careful around precarious drop-offs. Who doesn't need to know that? But anchoring in my mind a real worry about even going near any kind of edge by punishing me? Definitely overkill. (Pardon the pun.)

In this chapter, we're going to explore the *limiting beliefs* that have been ingrained in you by well-meaning parents, family members, friends, your individual culture and even yourself. We'll examine your *I can'ts* and your *I shouldn'ts,* asking questions that will take you beneath surface acceptance of those beliefs:

- Who says you can't or shouldn't?
- Are you taking the easy way out by listening to those beliefs?
- Is that limiting belief a hurdle to climb over, or is it a signpost that says, *Divert and keep going* or *Take a different path but don't stop moving*?
- Is this an artificial boundary which tells you that you're not good enough?

It's tough to turn those questions off entirely, but we'll talk in this chapter about how to change the effect they have on you. You might resist this at first, but one of the truly valuable lessons we learn from our parents is, *How do you know it won't work unless you try it?* (Though in my case that usually applied to some kind of suspicious food.) Give it a shot.

I offer two caveats before we begin.

One: Just because you don't have any crippling fears doesn't mean you should skip this chapter. When I say "fear" I'm including being a little scared, feeling anxious, experiencing laziness and habitually procrastinating. Those are all related to being frightened and can be about anything from fear of open spaces (agoraphobia) to choosing to be a couch potato and calling yourself innately lazy. If you can say you have none of those going on ever, you're not human!

Two: don't expect immediate, wholesale change. You've spent years running into those limiting beliefs and beating yourself up when you turn back. It's going to take intention every day to bring down those obstacles. As always, it's about baby steps. If that image doesn't work for you, try thinking of this as compounding interest on your savings. The interest doesn't seem like much at first, but over time it adds more and more to your nest egg. I think that resonates with all of us.

Tools for Facing the Fears

In Chapter Ten, I talked about the sides people typically come down on when it comes to being afraid:

- Some look at doubts and fears objectively so they can decide whether to push through, try a different route or back off entirely

- Others' doubts practically paralyze them, like demons hissing in their heads and making them immobile. There is no pushing through. There is only turning tail and running – if they can move at all.

Most of us don't fall entirely on one side or the other. Where you land depends on the situation and which limiting beliefs come into play. When we're talking about the big things – like this journey you've embarked on – the doubts tend to be more demon-like, simply because this *is* so important to you. The higher the stakes, the louder the fears.

To avoid going into either flight or freeze mode, it's best to equip yourself with certain tools. There are three I'd like you to consider in your journaling.

Tool #1. The courage to recognize what your fears are. Society constantly sends messages like "Just do it!" and "No Fear!" which make us feel like wimps if we can't embrace those slogans – so we don't admit that we even *have* fears. At first we 'fake it 'til we make it', and eventually we start believing in the non-existence of anything fearful in ourselves. Until one of them falls from the ceiling on top of us and we run from the room shrieking.

So, yeah, it does take a certain amount of bravery to own what you're afraid of, to look it in the face and name it. Seeing it for what it is can be fraught with a whole array of more demons.

- Looking at it squarely can involve dredging up painful memories. And as I've pointed out before, remembering something traumatic or disturbing creates the same kind of reaction in your brain and your body as experiencing it in the first place. Your palms sweat. Your heart races. You want to throw up everything you've eaten all day. No wonder you don't want to go there in your head.

- Going deep into fear may mean seeing yourself in a light you're not crazy about. When I was in the throes of the worst of the Rwenzori climb, I became very afraid I was going to succumb to the altitude, get sick and not be able to complete the journey. Hence, failure. Fearless adventurer that I was – or saw myself to be – I had a hard time admitting to myself I was concerned. Even now, I'm hedging. I wasn't just concerned; I was straight-up scared.

- If you're really attached to that fear, even thinking about it can be depressing and demoralizing. *I've never been able to overcome it before,* you tell yourself, *so why should this time be any different? I'm a loser (a wuss, a failure, a coward* – you fill in the blank).

Right now, all you need is the willingness. I'll take you through the process of overcoming the fears of this journey in a way that allows for some two steps forward, one step back. We'll make our way carefully, but make our way we will.

Tool #2: The courage to make a choice. You always have the freedom to say, *Yes, I want to get past that fear* or *No,*

I think I'll leave this alone for now. Just deciding between the two takes guts. Cowards don't know themselves well enough to be able to make a wise decision.

Here's an example. Nancy, my co-writer, has an intense fear of snakes. She finds the way they move, the way their tongues flicker and the potential some of them have to kill you terrifying. That fear has been fed by coming across these reptiles not once but twice *inside her home*, the last one a venomous copperhead. So is she at all interested in overcoming her phobia of these slithery, shoulderless creatures? Not even a little bit. She has no plans to visit a jungle – ever. Her house has been snake-proofed. So there is absolutely no reason to attempt a 'cure' for that fear.

However, let's say you want to spread the word about bullying. Your journey is to start a movement for safety and security for our kids in schools. That's going to mean doing presentations in those schools, at education boards, before administrators and parents, but you are deathly afraid of public speaking. Now that's a problem. This is a fear that needs to be addressed, or you can't possibly move forward.

That choice isn't quite as scary as you may be imagining. If you're familiar with exposure therapy, you know that it involves helping people heal from their phobias by putting them in a position where what they fear most is right in front of them. The goal is to show them that this thing they are so afraid of is not going to kill them, maim them or render them insane. But a person who is claustrophobic is not going to be immediately placed in an elevator and left there until he gets over it. That isn't therapy, that's cruelty, and no competent therapist does that.

Exposure therapy takes place in small increments over time. The client is not moved to the next stage until he or she can tolerate the current one. That might mean, in stage one, the therapist sits closer and closer to the client. Stage two could be the two of them sitting in a smaller room together. Stage three maybe involves a large closet. You get the idea. Eventually the client will be able to ride in that elevator without having a panic attack. Might there be nervousness still in play? Sure. But the courage to make the choice to confront leads to the confidence to overcome.

Another practice, which I much prefer, is disassociating yourself. Watch yourself watching yourself on a cinema screen. Play the video of your fear in full colour and sound. After the fear section has passed, stop immediately and rewind at high speed while playing ridiculous music and adding silly voices. Play it through again, stop, rewind faster but turn the colours and sounds down to black and white. Do this a few times and then return to your 'seat'. All the time, you are watching yourself watching yourself, which detaches you somewhat. Processing this way allows you to rationally park the fear.

Tool #3. The motivation to do something about it. It's one thing to choose to face the fear and another to actually take the steps. If public speaking is your personal hell, getting over it is going to mean eventually talking in front of people, even if you are certain you're going to pass out right there at the podium. If you have a deep fear of confrontation and people are trying to block your journey, getting past that is going to take learning how to stand tall and stick to your convictions. It's not just *Hey, I have this fear and I own it and I'm willing to deal with it.* We're talking, *I'm going to do whatever it takes to work through it.* That's a higher level of courage. It doesn't mean you're not afraid. It just means you're going to do it anyway.

Ready to try it?

The Three Questions for Facing Your Fears

Question #1. Who or what are the demons who frequently show up to scare you off from what you want to do?

You'd think they'd be easy to recognize, but most of us keep them so firmly under wraps we don't know they're there until they jump out and block the way – teeth bared and claws extended. So how do you ferret them out?

First, you have to know what fear feels like *before* it goes into attack mode. To determine how to describe this to you, I tried an experiment.

I put myself in a situation that I'd been procrastinating on. For this book to get into your hands, I had to come up with a marketing strategy. As you know, I have flip charts for everything else (four for the book alone), but I'd put off even starting a flip chart for how I was going to promote not just the book but all the parts of my vision that surround it. I told myself it was because

I know nothing about marketing, but I suspected there was some fear involved.

I began my experiment by letting myself feel scared about it. I imagined all this journey was going to entail and allowed the fear to happen. I'll get to what happened in a moment.

Then I gave myself permission to be lazy about it, to just shrug my shoulders and tell myself I didn't have the energy. What happened was interesting. More below.

I felt like I was onto something, so I reimagined other fear-based situations I'd been in – from being on the glacier on the mountain seeing my life flash before my eyes to not being bothered to go to the gym in favour of heading home and hitting the couch.

What I discovered will probably surprise you: there was a similarity between the feelings of fear and the feelings of procrastination. That was the *inner voice* telling me not to do whatever I was facing. Give that a go yourself, if you want, and see what happens.

No, I am not schizophrenic, and neither are you if there are familiar voices in your head. I have yet to meet anyone who doesn't have them. That main voice may sound like someone from your past. In my case, it's clearly my mum, nagging at me (just as she did out loud when I was growing up – and sometimes still does):

Why can't you just be normal?

Why can't you just settle down?

Why don't you do something safe?

I have to interject here that I love my mum and all she has done for me, my kids and the rest of the family. She would drop everything and come to any one of us at a time of crisis. Come to think of it, she loves a crisis! But in a normal, non-critical situation, she can still be the voice of limiting beliefs.

I used to think there was something wrong with me because I heard Mum's voice even when she was miles away. That was, until I recognized that what I 'heard' was actually me chatting to myself, and much of the time it was taking me along the path of least resistance. *Do something normal (whatever THAT is ...) Just settle down and stop going from adventure to adventure. Do something safe. Enough with putting yourself in harm's way.*

I also realized the sound turned up at moments when I least expected it. It arrived to give me advice I wasn't looking for, and certainly not advice that was going to help me through.

Now, let me be clear: there is also the inner voice that supports you. That keeps you going. That encourages you. But that voice sounds much different from the 'demon speech' I'm referring to. Which leads me to my question for you:

What does your fear voice SOUND like in your head?
For me, it has a nagging quality – sort of like a fingernail on a chalkboard. Yours might be angry, maybe even shouting. Or it could have the tenor of being afraid itself – whimpering, cowering, whining. Or perhaps it's coldly accusing.

It also helps to determine *who* it might sound like. I've been open about mine being a dead ringer for my mum.

That's common, and so is the father voice. That wretched teacher you had in Grade 5 is a likely candidate, as is the coach who browbeat you in secondary school, the sibling who bullied you mercilessly growing up (and still tries to) or the former spouse who did a number on your self-esteem in your time together. You may not be able to personify the voice this way, but if you can, it helps you realize its presence the moment it starts up.

Right now, in your journal, take some time to describe the voice that may have started as someone else in your past and has become the tape that plays in your head. If you can't pinpoint where it came from, give it a face and a name, but most important, observe how it sounds to you. In detail. Yes, those are your ideas the voice is expounding on, but it takes you to a bad neighbourhood of thought where you hang out with the wrong kind of influences. You have to know what those influences are, or you really can't move forward.

If you have vivid audio of your limiting inner voice, you're a third of the way to being able to turn it down. Let's go further with that.

Question #2. What do you currently do when fear/ anxiety/laziness/ procrastination shows up in that voice?
The possibilities are as numerous as people on the planet, but most reactions fall somewhere in this range:
- Do nothing. Freeze. Pretend it isn't there. Wait for it to go away.

- Actively avoid the thing. Hide from it. Do something else to distract yourself.
- Close off completely. From everything. Isolate. Stay there until you're sure the coast is clear, even if that means becoming a little paranoid.
- Panic. Freak all the way out. Become hysterical until somebody does something, dammit.
- Allow the demons to control your behaviour. Lash out. Hurt somebody. Hurt yourself.

Parts of some of those can be good in the short term, depending on the situation. As I write this, the world is in the midst of the COVID-19 pandemic. We are right to be at least concerned that we will contract this virus, so we are staying in our homes, shutting ourselves off from this illness that can kill.

But if it's something potentially good you're fearful of, none of those reactions are going to get you where you long to be. What you are dodging will only come back in the future, with interest, and destroy at least the moment, if not the entire journey.

I can attest to that. I climbed a number of heights before my Rwenzori experience, so you'd think I'd have been a completely confident person in all areas of my life. Not so. For instance, I've had many experiences where I couldn't – literally could not – speak out at a meeting because I didn't understand the extraordinary vocabulary that was being bandied about. Many times that voice has told me I'm inadequate, stupid and uneducated and to just keep my mouth shut.

I've learned how to get past that, which leads us to our next question. But before we go there, carve out some time to do this in your journal:

1. First, in your mind, take yourself back to a time when fear got its icy fingers around your neck. It doesn't have to be something that would terrify just about anybody. Just you. If what comes to you is on a par with a recent confrontation with a spider, a toe-to-toe with your mother-in-law or a dressing-down by your supervisor, you're on the right track. Feel the fear. If you're using a situation where you procrastinated but didn't call it fear at the time – dragged your feet on paying your taxes, couldn't bring yourself to practise your yoga, 'neglected' to tell your significant other about the total on the credit card bill – feel the emotions and the physical ramifications of putting something off. Write it down.

2. Then remember how you *reacted* when you felt those feelings. Be honest. Nobody else has to know that you flipped out because you thought someone was breaking into your house when it was a branch blowing against the window. Just record your reaction in your journal.

3. Finally, have a think about whether you were happy with the way you handled your fear. Once a scare subsides, there is a tendency to feel sheepish, ashamed, embarrassed by your knee-jerk actions. Or maybe you told yourself you were justi-

fied in lashing out, freaking out or passing out. If you already have a pretty good handle on most of your fears, and you can say, *Good job!*, try picking a different situation. Remember that pretending the fear didn't happen is a reaction itself.

Keep your journal handy as you go on to the next question.

Question #3. How can you move past that fear?

If you knew how to do that, you'd be doing it already, right? Most of us need some coaching on this, so here's what I have for you:

- **Try doing the opposite of what your fear tells you to do.** This applies when you have determined that the fear is holding you back rather than giving you a wise warning. If the voice says, *This guy has a criminal record, an even worse track record with relationships, and he has no visible means of financial support,* listen when it tells you to run from that potential relationship as fast as you can. No, we're talking here about continuing to return to an abusive significant other because you're afraid of being alone. Not wanting to face a business situation you've never encountered before because the fear of making a fool of yourself is enormous. Cancelling plans with new acquaintances because you're afraid they'll reject you once they start getting to know you.

In those cases, **do the opposite.**

Say no, you're not going back to the abuser. You deserve better. You're awesome and you won't be alone forever.

Ask for advice with that business situation from someone you trust. It isn't a sign of stupidity that you don't already know everything. Who does?

Go meet those potential new friends. Ask them questions about themselves. Appreciate their good qualities. It will come back to you in kind, and if it doesn't, those are not people you want as mates anyway.

Being brave doesn't mean donning a shield and full military kit. You aren't going into battle with your fear. You're just thanking it for its input and doing the very thing it's telling you not to do.

That results in as powerful a feeling as slaying a giant. Actually, it *is* slaying a giant!

- **Ask yourself, "What is the worst that can happen if I do this?"** I'm sure you've heard that before. I certainly didn't invent it. And you may be thinking that imagining the worst possible scenario is only going to give you an anxiety attack. But at this point, after the work you've already done in this chapter, it just might make sense to you this time.

Rather than mentally experiencing those scenarios, detach from them, observe them as if they're happening to someone else and record them in your journal.

Let's take going to the gym, since that is unlikely to conjure up fire-breathing dragons in your head. You've defined your journey as getting fit. You've taken the first steps on your flip chart. You've bought the gym membership, purchased the right clothes and you've actually gone there with gusto. Every day at first. Then a few times a week, because you were tired the other days. Or because you have to park your car and walk a bit to get into the gym and it's freakin' cold out there. And now? You're going home after work most nights and joining that demon, Procrastination, and his cousin, Laziness, on the couch. In fact, you can't remember the last time you did work out. That brand of fear has won. Journey over.

For the moment.

What is the worst that could happen if you said to those demons, "You know what? It's easier hanging out here with you, but I'm sick of doing 'easy'. Tonight, I'm going back in there and restarting this thing."

You'll look like a wimp next to all those fit bodies.

You won't see results immediately.

You'll miss that episode of your current TV obsession.

The couch won't get used as much.

I'm not seeing anything on that list that could do you any harm. Quite the reverse, in fact.

That leads us to the next list to make in your journal. What is the *best* that could happen if you face down that fear that masquerades as laziness?

You'll eventually see results.

You'll realize that 'wimp' only describes people who do nothing. Just walking through the door shows strength and good old-fashioned guts.

You'll no longer look in the mirror and see a body you don't want. You'll see one you actually like being in.

You'll feel more energetic.

And, best of all, *you won't be able to call yourself a lazy procrastinator, because you won't be one.*

When I was frozen on the glacier near Margherita Peak, you'll recall, I considered just letting myself fall over the edge and ending the misery. I didn't consciously think, *What is the best that could happen if I choose to keep going?* But I knew what that best thing was: I would see my daughters again. In fact, I *had* to see them. And that eliminated all the *Worst Things* that could happen if I tried to navigate that glacier.

Your *The Worst That Can Happen* list might be a little more frightening than the gym example I've used (and less so than me on the glacier!). That spouse you're leaving might not take no for an answer. That boss you reach out to for advice might rethink his decision to give you the task he's trusted you with. Those people you want to befriend could ditch you after that first get-together at the pub.

So you ...

- **Take one small step.** You don't have to defeat the fear all at once. You probably couldn't if you tried.

Anxious in a meeting where everyone is talking over your head? One step can be putting your hand up and saying you don't understand. You might not be the only one in the room who doesn't.

Feeling like a lazy slob because you gave up the gym? One step can be to just go back one time. Work out for thirty minutes. See how it feels.

Afraid your boss will think you're incompetent because you have to ask for help? One step might be looking for someone else to give you advice. Or telling your boss what you do feel comfortable with and saying, *But I have one question.*

Take that single step, and here's what will happen: you'll feel a little more confident because you didn't run away, have an anxiety attack or actually die. That confidence will allow you to take the next step, which will empower you even more. This is compounding interest. One step builds on another until you are rockin' it on your journey again.

And this doesn't apply to your current goal alone. On future paths, when the fear voice begins to hiss or nag or scream at you, instead of giving up at the first sign of it, you'll know what to do: do the opposite. Imagine the worst that could happen, none of which probably will. Imagine the best that could happen and take the first step toward it.

Action

Let's apply this to a fear you named in Question #1. You can start with a lesser one or go straight for the jugular and choose your biggest. In your journal, write down and fill in the following:

1. Name the fear _____
   _____

2. What is the fear telling you NOT to do?
   _____
   _____

3. What is the opposite of what your fear is telling you?
   _____
   _____

4. What one thing could you do to take action on that opposite?
   _____
   _____

5. List the worst things that could happen if you take that action:
   _____
   _____
   _____
   _____

6. Cross out the "worst things" that will not injure or kill you or cause you to lose your mind. (That will probably be all of them)

7. What is one small step you could take to complete 4. above?
   _____
   _____

8. When will you do that?
   _____
   _____

9. **Put it on your calendar**
10. **Do it**
11. **Record how you feel in your journal**
12. **Repeat Steps 1–11 with every fear**

Time to Move On to the Next Phase?

When is it time to turn to Chapter Seventeen and learn how to reach your peak? The obvious answer is when you don't feel too afraid or too lazy to move forward. But notice the qualifying word "too". You're likely to feel somewhat nervous, uneasy, pensive, a little unsure, a bit tentative – at least until you've compounded some interest in your confidence account. If you're experiencing new energy and poise and you're genuinely eager to continue the journey, then, yes, it's time.

But what if the scary stuff lingers and you become nauseous when you even think about encountering it around the next corner? That's probably because you're still imagining the worst. If that's your M.O., try this exercise. Read the instructions until you see ... Then pause to follow them before you move on to the next prompt.

Imagine that you're sitting in a prison cell. Experience your surroundings with all your senses. The rancid smells, the cold steel sounds, the angry air, the shadows cast by the bars, the taste of hopelessness in your mouth ...

Now imagine throwing yourself at the door of the cell, gripping the bars and shouting for someone to let you out ...

The guard saunters up and tells you that all you have to do to be free is go over to the cabinet on the cell wall and break the glass door. Inside you'll find a key to let yourself out.

Imagine how that feels! Freedom is just within your reach ...

See yourself diving to that cabinet, your shoe in your hand to break the glass, and coming to an abrupt halt. The sign on the door says *Your Worst Fears Inside*. The guard didn't tell you that part. To get to the key to your freedom, you have to let out your worst *fears*? Experience how it feels to have that decision to make: do you remain imprisoned by your fears, or do you take a chance, break the glass, grab the key and run for your life? ...

If at this point, your real self is saying, *WHAT decision? Break the glass! Who cares what comes out?*, you are ready to move forward.

If you're hesitating, look at the wall above the still-locked cabinet. There's a sign there that says *Break Glass in Emergency Only*. Let me tell you, there is no bigger emergency than finding out that you have imprisoned yourself. And there is no fear worth keeping yourself there.

In your mind, break the glass ... Take the key ... Open that creaky door and step out. Walk confidently down the corridor, past the guards ...

Some of them might say, *Took you long enough*. Others may tell you, *You'll be back*. Still others could call out, *Good on ya! You can do this!* It really doesn't matter. All you're focusing on is the bright light of the free world.

You're headed for those doors, and nothing is going to stop you ...

If you can't see yourself doing that, it's okay. Stay with this chapter and work with it until you can.

If you *can* imagine that kind of freedom and you want it more than anything, you are ready to head for the peak.

CHAPTER SEVENTEEN

REACHING THE PEAK

FOCUS. FOCUS. FOCUS.

That word drove me onward and upward toward Margherita Peak. It was the word that led me to take every step carefully. That had me ask the important questions:

How strong is that last ledge?

Will this ice axe stop me from plummeting off the mountain?

What do I have to do to stay with each step?

Despite the cold, I was hot and sweaty. The weather battered me. The images of reaching the top flew around in my mind. But the inner command – *Keep going* – came from that one word.

Focus. Focus. Focus.

My focus was on the goal. I was making my way toward it one step at a time. Toward that beautiful image of success. The top.

And then I was there.

If you'll recall from Chapter Eleven, I suddenly looked around me and realized I was at the peak. All that build-up (literally!), and without fanfare I was on the top of Mount Stanley. Oddly, after all we'd been through, I asked myself –

How did that happen?

How am I here so quickly?

Is this all there is? Is this it?

But the strangest question of all, the one I was totally unprepared for was this:

Now what?

I was almost literally on top of the world – in that region we were – and I should have been figuratively as well. Granted, there was little time to celebrate. We couldn't linger or there would be no daylight for our descent, and melting snow and ice on the glacier were making it more treacherous than it already was. But in addition, the view couldn't compare to what I expected. The feeling of exhilaration I'd anticipated didn't happen. I'd planned, prepared and struggled past every hurdle there was to reach that goal. And now just ... the end?

Eventually, that climb did change my life, and we'll get to that in our last two chapters. At that moment, though, I couldn't see it. The attainment of what I'd strived so hard for seemed anticlimactic.

Ever felt that anticlimax before? After all your struggle and hard work, all you have been working for suddenly appears and you find yourself asking. "Oh, is this it?" And saying, "I was expecting something more." Of course, maybe you don't stop at the peak at all. Maybe you just carry on seeing this achievement as no big deal.

It can actually be even worse than that. People who have worked and trained and studied for years for something commonly become depressed at worst, and restless at the least, after reaching a major goal. We have heard of Olympic athletes who go home after winning multiple gold medals, having achieved their biggest life goal, only to sink into despair and lose all the benefits of their wins. It isn't unusual for medical students to go into a funk once that M.D. is firmly attached to their names. Or actors who have won Oscars and Tonys to flail around looking for a new role.

It's worse than the day after Christmas.

Add to that the fact the journey is really only half-done. In my case every foot we had to climb to get up to the peak we now had to descend to get back home. There was something demoralizing about that. About being at another starting line.

But it doesn't have to be that way, and I don't want it to be for you. You, too, have prepared and journeyed and overcome fears and setbacks. You deserve to recognize what you've achieved and be proud. And not just proud, but motivated. Once that success is in you, you see yourself as successful, which stacks up future victories and accomplishments and milestones and makes you ready to take on anything you want to do.

To get you there, in this chapter I'll lead you through several mini-phases, if you will, in this experience of being near the peak.

- How you feel about being successful. What you discover may surprise you.

- What success on *this* journey looks like. What will it take for you to say, "I have done it. I'm there"?
- How to fully celebrate your success. I couldn't do that at the peak, but I did later, and I'm glad I didn't scoot past it. It can make all the difference.

Although we're going to examine that last one more fully later in the chapter, I'd like for you to try an exercise right now. This is best done when no one else is around, so if you're sitting on a train or in a coffee shop or a doctor's office waiting room, you might want to put this off until you're alone. Otherwise, you're bound to get strange looks which may say, *Have you lost it?!*

1. Hold your arms up above your head. Go on, just do it.

2. Look up as if you have won the race and shout, "Yes!" Okay, you can whisper it if that's more your personality, but say it. Out loud.

3. You will feel a wave of emotion sweep through you, even though you have not, in fact, just won a competition. If you don't feel anything, try it again. Feel it? Close your eyes and *then* look up and say, "Yes!" See?

All you did was *simulate* success and you felt some sense of power. Imagine – truly, close your eyes and imagine – how amazing you will feel when you *do* hit your summit and you raise your arms and shout. The shivers of excitement, the recognition of what you have achieved will be anchored in your body.

Repeatedly anchoring success only increases those feelings. Think of the last thing you achieved, even if it seems relatively minor. You went to the gym for the first time in six months. You got through an entire evening without yelling at your kids. You kept your temper in a confrontation with your boss. Whatever the accomplishment, see it as success. Raise your arms and shout, "Yes!"

Keep doing that every time you overcome an obstacle or reach an objective, no matter how small. The energy that comes from recognizing success this way is uplifting. Your body position changes. Your head position alters. Your shoulders no longer slump. That fizz of excitement reaches the extremities, your fingertips and toes. It vitalizes the whole body like an electric shock. You stand tall because you can achieve. You *have* achieved. And you will go on building a library of success.

Shall we give it a go?

Tools for Reaching the Peak

Tool #1. Some real-life images that keep you focused, motivated.

For me, that was my daughters. Remember me talking about the memories of the Sunday Night Fight Night which kept me hanging on and moving forward when I was tempted to let go? Your images may be of important people in your life too – not those you want to prove something to, but those who encourage you, the ones you want to make proud. The first person on that list should be you.

For some people this is a spiritual image. For others, an actual award or financial gain. For still others we may be talking about an anticipated feeling, perhaps of pride or confidence or wholeness. In the case of the latter, a symbol might be in order. What does pride or confidence or wholeness look like to you?

Just be ready with pictures in your mind that will spur you on. You'll see why as we progress through the chapter.

Tool #2. A way to capture the emotions/experiences as they arise.

The journal you've been using is perfect for this. Set up a section and have pen at the ready. The little sparks, the surges of hope, the first glimpse of the top need to be written down or photographed. This not only chronicles the journey but marks the steps, which energizes you. Looking not at how far you have to go but at how far you've come is a boost you'll need.

Tool #3. As always, a willingness to take a good look at yourself.

The very first question below will take you on a side-trip into yourself which may stir up some old stuff. Unless you get that up and out, it will be difficult to make that peak. You have nothing to lose by doing this, and everything to gain. If it helps, no one has to know what you uncover but you.

Let's start there.

The Three Questions for Reaching the Peak

Question #1. If anything is going to hold you back from taking those last steps, what is it likely to be?
In Chapter Sixteen we talked about the fears and limiting beliefs that might stand in your way as you *begin* the journey. At this point you've hopefully taken enough steps on your way to your goal to have recognized that those fears are unfounded. What we're talking here are the specific doubts and misgivings that can keep you from taking the *final* steps, even after you have come so far.

That may seem absurd on the surface. Why would you give up when the peak is in sight? Actually, people do it all the time.

- The person who works hard to get a project off the ground, only to walk away just before launch, leaving someone else to get the credit
- The one who works hard, gets to the goal, but then feels too shy to be recognized for that achievement. This is, after all, just part of the job.
- The winner who questions whether she deserves to win. Or who worries that other people might think he's a grandstander.
- The would-be writer who receives encouragement from an agent and is told to send in the book when it's completed. And then all writing stops.
- The couple who have saved for years to make a down payment on a house but can't make a choice on which property to buy.
- Fill in your own: _____

_____

What makes a person throw in the towel when the end, the reward, the top, is within his or her grasp?

Fear of the unknown – and in this case, that unknown is success.

Again, this appears ridiculous at first glance. But let's dig a little deeper.

I think we can all agree that fear of failure can prevent us from *starting* a journey. That makes a certain kind of sense. However, it is fear of succeeding that can keep us from *finishing.* The reasons for that are unique to every person, but in general they arise from these kinds of things:

- Life is going to be different once you've reached that goal. That means leaving the comfort zone, and whatever kind of rut you've been in, it's *your* rut. It's familiar. You know how to behave there. But attaining success can carry with it fear of the consequences. Will you have to be in the limelight, which terrifies you? Will you be the centre of attention, which freaks you out? Will you make more money, which you aren't necessarily good at handling? Will it be embarrassing? Are you even ready for it?

- You obviously want whatever it is you're climbing toward. But once that success is looming, you may wonder whether you deserve it. Will you get there and find out you're a complete fake? The 'imposter syndrome' is a real thing, an internalized fear of being exposed as a fraud, despite external evidence of your competence. It appears in the mind as, "When are they going to find out I really don't know what I'm doing?"

- Does success seem selfish to you? Are you afraid you'll push someone else out of the way? Forget to give credit? Become all about your own advancement, something you despise in other people? In the past, have you been in the habit of getting so far and then handing the whole thing over to someone else so they can get the glory?

Whether you can relate to any of those or have thought of others that are currently pulling at your shirt tail as you have the summit within reach, it is very easy to sabotage yourself. To decide you've left something out in a previous step and scurry back to make things perfect before you try for the top again. To get stuck in the minutia or, worse, the terror of being in all-new territory.

Just as you mapped out your journey and overcame your fears so you could get started, you can draw a new map and defeat success phobia so you can keep going. With your journal in front of you, complete the following self-discovery steps. This is not a pause in your climb; it is a very necessary part of it.

A. Think of a time when you were afraid of success and got in your own way or handed over the reins at the final furlong. Write down the situation.

B. Go back to the very start of that sabotaging process. What did it *feel* like when you first began to put the brakes on? Describe the physical manifestations. Butterflies in your gut? All-over anxiety? Fatigue?

C. What did you *think* when you started experiencing those feelings? How did you convince yourself that giving up or handing it over was a good idea? *I'm not ready for this. I won't be the best person to represent this to the public. I think this is too self-serving.*

D. What *action* did you take – or not take? Did you take steps to turn the job over to someone else? Step down from your position? Just sort of let it fade away?

E. What did you *tell yourself* about why you were backing off? Did you make up a story in your head about needing to stop so you could spend more time with your family, get your financial affairs in order, take better care of your health?

Once you've completed that, make a more succinct list in your journal of four things that happen to you when success is on the horizon, following B through E above. Here's an example:

1. I start to get uneasy, and it's hard to concentrate.
2. I think about the attention I'm going to receive, and I almost panic.
3. I talk to people about how unready I feel to take that on until I find someone who agrees with me.
4. I tell myself this is better for everybody. I would probably make a mess out of it anyway.

If you just skipped that exercise, seriously consider going back and completing it. We have to understand what we're doing, what we're saying internally when we cut ourselves off from the success we want. Seeing that clearly is the key to going for the goal line anyway, despite the palpable fear of succeeding. Get that information down in your journal and then move on to the next step.

Take the time to thank yourself for understanding you – the things that make you an obstacle to achieving what you so deeply long for. Seriously, write a thank you in your journal, just as you would to a mentor or friend who helped you see reason. Ironically, it takes courage to face your lack of it. You've done that. Write it down and then raise your arms, look up and say, "Yes!"

Have I actually done that? Absolutely. In the writing of this book, I've feared success a number of times. I may help millions of people be the best they can be, yes, but I will be centre stage (hopefully!). Do I want that? I have a story to tell and I'm telling it, and yet ...

I did just what I'm advising you to do: create a way to recognize how amazing you truly are. Use mine or write your own statement that is filled with I am, I will, I have.

I am loved. I approve of myself. I am amazing.
I have all the skills, abilities and power to notice,
overcome and truly achieve. Yes, there will be the
naysayers. I just say thank you to them as I look
to the future and try it on for size.

Do I walk around expounding those virtues to anyone who happens to be standing close by? Of course not. But I have to know them. And I have to be grateful for them.

Here is the logic behind that. Journeys are actually you competing with yourself. Even if the goal seems external – a promotion, an improved relationship, a degree, a place on the team – the real success is in the fact that you have dug deep. You. Not anyone else with an opinion. This is about you kicking your own ass.

So yeah, that deserves some appreciation.

Next, commit to changing those four things you listed. Actually write a statement of commitment in your journal. It could be something like: *In spite of my misgivings about making it to the finish line, I will put those voices to bed and I will get past whatever I have to within myself to get there.* Putting it in writing makes it real. It gives you something to come back to if the self-sabotaging tries to overtake you again.

Committed to that change, do the following. Again, writing your answers in your journal anchors success as much as physically raising your arms and whispering, "Yes." Or if you want to reinforce more – write it on a Post-it, stick it on the mirror and read it aloud daily.

This will be familiar to you: you're going to do the opposite of what you usually do to trip yourself up just when victory is in sight.

Change the sound of the inner voice. It's speaking loud and clear right now, and you'd have a hard time shutting it up. So put another voice in its place. A louder one. A clearer one. A positive one. And one that makes a heck of a lot more sense.

Old voice: You are not going to be able to handle this. You're terrible in front of an audience.

New voice: I deserve every bit of this, I have put the effort in. I know my topic more than anyone and I will share this with others.

If you want to write it down just that way, go for it. However you put it into words on paper, it will give you experience in replacing negative thoughts with positive ones. Ones that are actually true.

Change the narrative. Instead of telling yourself stories about what a hot mess you're going to make of this whole thing, revisualize the vision you had of this journey back in the beginning. Do it in a layered way, as follows.

1. Write your vision in a few sentences. See it in black and white.
2. Next, read it out loud. Once you've said it, the vision becomes more real, especially if, as you say it you look upwards and see the words come to life above you.
3. Finally, imagine yourself feeling the success you'll arrive at when you reach the top. If the arm-raising motion helps you, do that. Or simply watch and hear the vision as if it is happening. An emotion will well up.

Just as with everything else I've suggested to you, I have absolutely done that too. I have envisioned myself on stage, probably wearing smart jeans, a T-shirt and a jacket. There is a packed audience, so I have to use one of those fancy microphones that comes round the side of my face to my mouth. There I am, telling this story, sharing what will benefit those listening to me. The vision ends with my kids rushing out from the wings to join me and my eyes glazing as I hold back those tears, because without them none of this would be real.

For me, that's amazing. Even as I write this, I can feel the shimmer of achievement.

And the purpose of that exercise is ...?

Each time you overlay another sense over your vision, you create something more real. As we've said before, your brain doesn't know the difference between experiencing the actual event and imagining the event. It performs the same way in both situations. Think about the last time you were really angry about something. Say it out loud. Ten to one you can *feel* that anger all over again.

Therefore, enacting your success in your mind makes it easier to achieve because your brain thinks you already have. If you do it once, you can surely do it again, right?

You might have to go a little deeper if you have found yourself thinking, *I don't deserve this success.* I could simply ask you the question, *Why not you?* but I don't think that will help you much. It might even reinforce the negative thinking that got you there in the first place. Instead, let's take a positive approach.

In your journal, give three reasons why you *do* deserve this success. Stay with it until you can come up with all three. Do NOT tell yourself you're being full of yourself. This isn't about conceit. This is about facing your own strengths. No successful person ever reached the peak by practising false humility.

An example for you:

1. I've worked my backside off for this. I've earned it!
2. I'm doing this for some very generous reasons. This is going to make a difference in other people's lives. I'm a good person.
3. I've helped a lot of other people attain their success. It is my turn.

Before you move on to the next question, write in your journal anything that has come to you as you've worked with Question 1 which you want to ponder and remember. That could include things that still trip you up. Doubts that continue to niggle at you. But you can – and should – also make note of positive ideas that have come to you. Maybe you have a clearer picture of where you're headed than you did before you completed the exercises. Could be you feel somewhat stronger. Write it down.

Question #2. What if the view from the top doesn't look exactly the way you envisioned it?

The fear of being disappointed is enough for some people to give the whole thing up completely. I didn't anticipate feeling let down on reaching Margherita Peak, but for a moment I did. The view didn't match the drone footage we'd seen of a perfect environment. I'd looked forward to great views, blue sky, fresh, clean mountain air. My vision had included a celebratory photograph of the four of us with our guides I could print later and be proud of.

Yeah. What we found was a white, frozen, craggy picture of hell. The wind was howling. To say it was freezing is an understatement. The very cold, beaten-up bodies, no view, no azure sky – that was what we captured in a quick snapshot next to the sign. It was hard to enjoy the victory when all I wanted to do was get out of there.

Fortunately, I didn't leave it at that. In the midst of the cloudy view and the shivering body, one thought came to mind: *we made it.* And in that moment, the only thing that really mattered was that thought. *We made it.*

Saving the peak experience was a matter of stripping down to the basics.

What had I originally set out to do? What was my goal? To reach the highest point in Uganda. That was it. Yes, on the way I was battered by weather and beaten down by frightening thoughts. There on the peak I didn't see what I'd expected to see. But when I stripped it back, a perfect climb and a spectacular view were not part of my objective. I set out to simply reach the top, and I had.

This is a matter of not being too harsh on ourselves. If we get what we wanted when we set out, right down at its core, that is a success worth celebrating, even if all the details are not precisely as we envisioned them. The vision got us to the top. It didn't fail us. *We* did not fail.

What had I learned? It isn't enough to say, *I did it!* if we don't look at how we can do better next time. The disappointments can be overridden by the positive answer to that question. I'll be climbing another peak in a few months' time. I know now to be better prepared in terms of fitness and kit. I've learned to be ready for the negative voice that may try to take me down. That doesn't mean criticize all the things I did wrong. That's pointless. I did it, I learned from it and I will do it even better next time.

That is success.

Besides, it is human nature to get as much pleasure from anticipation as from the event we're looking forward to. What did you like better as a child – the enchanting season leading up to Christmas Day, or the day after when it seemed all the good stuff had already happened?

I've encouraged you to build up that anticipation by visualizing the journey and the peak. We as people love the build-up. We love creating a dream in our minds, with all the particulars. We might even overdramatize as we keep the image in the forefront of our minds. This is going to be great.

Without that image we probably wouldn't even begin. So I am not torturing you by having you layer the senses on your vision and make it amazing in your mind, only to have you let down. Getting there is indeed half the fun. Would you want to miss that interior journey?

If you keep your basic goal in mind as you reach the pinnacle, you can feel that same excitement even if absolutely everything doesn't play out the way you hoped. Try answering this question in your journal:

What is the most basic, fundamental thing that will make me be able to say, "I have done it, despite all these things that fall short of my total, perfect vision." State the very minimum.

Some examples might help:

- Goal: be promoted to the next level. Will that be enough even if not everybody supports me along the way? If it takes longer than I thought it would? If, when I get the promotion, I don't get the corner office? Can I still say, with arms raised, "Yes!"

- Goal: to have a showing of my creative work in an art gallery. Will I still feel successful if very few people show up? If people come but no one buys anything? If the lighting isn't exactly the way I want it? Can I still say, "I got a showing! That's huge! Success!"

- Goal: to be on speaking terms with my children. Will I feel good about it if we don't discuss anything beneath the surface? If we only talk once a week? If it feels a little stiff? If we talk once a week without ending up in a shouting match, can I still say, "I'm speaking to my children. I love that. Love. It."?

Keep in mind that this journey whose peak you're about to reach is one of many you will take. Some are journeys we make just to learn how to do a better job of it next time. It's worth stopping here to consider what I call *false peaks*.

If you've ever been near a mountain range or seen pictures or video footage of, say, the Himalayas or the US Rockies, you know there isn't just one peak. Any range is made up of a series of them. I was in the Rwenzori range. Mount Stanley, which I climbed, was only one mountain in that range, and Margherita, while the highest peak, was not the only peak.

I discovered that when you're walking or climbing up a mountain, you look up and see what you believe is the top. You approach that thinking, "Yeah, I'm nearly there!" But as you get closer to that top, the angle opens up and you can see that you have further to go. There are five or six more peaks ahead of you. Enoch is saying, "Just a little further," when you clearly see it's a *lot* further. This has the potential to be soul-destroying, unless you realize that reaching every peak is a success in itself. It lets you see that you've made it this far, and if you keep going the same way, you'll make it to the very top.

Applied to life, it seems to me that the summit of a particular journey may actually be one of those false peaks. But it is a peak. You have accomplished a great deal, and much that you can put into climbing to that next one. Seriously, when in life are we ever completely 'there'? I'm happy to accept these smaller summits as part of life's continuing journey.

Take the writing of this book. The goal of the journey is to tell the story. I'm doing that. When I type "The End", I will have reached the summit.

Of this journey.

But what good is a book if it isn't published? That will be another goal. If you are reading it, I reached that peak.

And what is the point of a published book if no one reads it? The next goal will be to get it into people's hands. The next *journey*, then, will be to create and execute a marketing plan.

If I had set my original goal as *Make my book a best-seller,* I might have already given up. Each part of that ultimate goal has to be seen as a journey in itself. This Successful Book mountain range has many peaks.

Now your turn.

If you are at the point in your journey where you think you see the summit above you, write in your journal the basic, fundamental thing that must be there when you arrive in order for you to say, *I've done it!* Leave out all the details of your vision and simply write down that original goal in its most basic terms. When you reach your peak, that means you *have* done it. It might not be pretty, and it definitely won't be perfect. But it will be success. Perhaps include the answers to these questions:

Am I prepared for some of the things I have envisioned to be absent or not up to par?

Can I be content with the bare minimum?

What might that mean in terms of future peaks?

If you have already reached that peak and you're disappointed that it feels rather of anticlimactic, write your original goal down in your journal. As you think back, know that the anticlimactic feeling is just those gremlins discouraging you from having another go at something similar in the future, but now you know better. You know they just want to chill on the sofa.

Write your answers to these questions:

Have I met that stripped-down goal?

How good does it really look?

What can I go on to achieve?

Could this be a 'false' peak? Is it exciting to know that I still have more to achieve? That this is only the beginning for me in this new way of living?

Question #3. How will you celebrate in a concrete, significant way?

Whether your peak is the ultimate one in a long journey or one of the 'false peaks' along the way, when you reach it, you owe it to yourself to celebrate. Not only will you get to experience that "Yes!" moment for real, but the feeling you have when you honour your achievement will be so satisfying, you'll want to live it again. And that will put you on a higher platform, ready to take on the next challenge.

When you think of the word 'celebrate', what comes to mind?

Some people immediately envision a bottle of champagne, a sumptuous feast, a gang of people all raising their glasses and proclaiming your awesomeness.

Others may see themselves retreating a little, relishing the success privately or with someone who was instrumental along the way. And then perhaps opening the hip flask and having a swig …

Unfortunately, there are also those who take only a moment to say, "Cool. Done," and then move on to the next target, taking no time at all to appreciate what they've achieved. I think this is a mistake. Without conscious recognition and some way to commemorate the victory, the reaching of a peak becomes just another job you had to do. A shrug and a new goal leads to the same kind of drudgery you were probably trying to change by setting the goal in the first place.

Think of it this way. If your goal was to lead a team to a certain peak (and maybe it was!), you would most likely put some thought into how to reward them. A team get-together. A bonus. Certificates of commendation for all. That would not only recognize the success but motivate the members to aim even higher in the next challenge. A mere "Thanks, and, oh, how are you getting on with that task I gave you ...?" isn't going to accomplish that. Recall how much the certificate I received at the end of the climb meant to me.

Why, then, would you not do the same thing for yourself? You don't have to throw a party, take everybody to dinner or splurge on an island vacation. You *can* do that, but what makes a good celebration doesn't involve spending a lot of money or making a splash. This is about you paying your respects to what you've done, not wrangling everybody else into doing it for you! Being a cocky, "Do you see how I did that?" kind of person rubs people the wrong way. Eventually, they just tolerate that person rather than like or respect them.

In fact, many, many times we must celebrate solo. As we'll discuss in Chapter Eighteen, not everyone will see what you've accomplished as anything significant. *We're going to the pub because you did what? Why is that a big deal?* The toasting of a peak reached is not so everyone can tell you how wonderful you are. It's for you to recognize that in yourself. Celebrate, yes. Just don't discount the benefits of doing it all on your own.

However you decide to do it, what are the qualities of a good celebration?

- *Something you're comfortable with.* This isn't the moment to shove yourself out of your comfort zone. If you love a party, go for it. If you like toasting yourself alone in front of a fire, do that thing. If you're more comfortable not doing anything at all, try journaling about that. Your reasons for not relishing your own accomplishments are probably deeply rooted. It's worth taking a look.

- *Something specific to what you've done.* If you got that promotion, why not treat yourself to a new personal gift befitting your new position (new briefcase, nice fountain pen ...)? If you had a showing of your artwork, could you invite your artist friends over and open a good bottle of wine? If you and your children are talking again, can you share that with someone who will get the significance?

Action

No matter how you choose to celebrate, absolutely do this: find a creative way to look at *HOW* you made it. If you've ever been part of a team that won a big game or a group that threw a successful party or even a few people who have gone through a difficult experience together, you know that one of the most satisfying parts of that is in the aftermath, when you all sit down and review together every highlight, then every step, then every tiny moment. Do that with your own reaching of the peak. Whether you write this in your journal, glass of bubbly in hand, or discuss it with a close friend who can enjoy both the talk and the starters you provide, ponder these questions:

What were the important things that got me to the peak?
What did I have to go through to get there?
What went wrong and right along the way?
What really felt good?
What can I learn from this experience?
What do I want to know before I start my next journey?

Time to Move On to the Next Phase?

Celebrating your success makes the journey so much richer. You still have a way to go before it's completed. As we realized earlier, the peak is actually the halfway point. But if you take the time to salute and mark your achievement, the rest of the way will be so much more rewarding.

How do you know you're ready to continue? And you do need to. There's more to be done. That pot is boiling, but it won't keep boiling unless you keep the heat up. If the kitchen metaphor doesn't work for you, maybe this one will.

Being at the peak, post-celebration, is like being at another starting line. Would you show up at a race, hand over a record of your training and say, "Right. I'm here. Where's my medal?" Strange looks, guaranteed.

You know it's time to start down the mountain when you're ready to do something with this success you've achieved. Getting the promotion isn't enough. Now you have to show what kind of job you can do in this position. Having a showing of your paintings is a start. Are you ready to learn from the critiques you received and go back into your studio? Talking to your children pleasantly twice a week is a good beginning. Is it time to broach some deeper topics with them?

You are the only one who can answer that question. You *know* the answer. You did the preparation, the mapping. You overcame your fears. You fundamentally reached your goal. You now have what it takes to begin at this next starting line, to make the climb down the mountain.

That's what creates a New You.

CHAPTER EIGHTEEN

DISCOVERING THE NEW YOU

WHEN I RETURNED HOME from the Rwenzori climb, I found the abundance too much: the almost embarrassing selection of food, the hectic movement of people, the speeding cars. I was truly grateful to be alive and seeing all those things again, but it was all overwhelming. I felt as if I'd been catapulted into a different world entirely.

That got me thinking about whether this frenetic pace was really the path for me. I realized I was working full-out yet not feeling I was getting anywhere. I wondered – did I need to change my focus and adopt a new approach to get the best out of my life? The answer was yes. Because the mountain had changed me.

Which is not actually surprising. I had watched life flash before me as I clung to that near-vertical glacier. Seeing myself at the various mental and physical lows during that climb forced me to re-evaluate what my life was really about, where I wanted to go with it, what I truly wanted to achieve.

There is definitely something about journeying to the top, overcoming fear and even experiencing closeness to death that calls into question who you are now. At least it did for me. Since then, even as I continue to move through life, I regularly reflect on how I can put into practice what I learned in that icy place, so that when anything difficult comes my way I can cut through it. But more importantly, the new person I am becoming as a result allows me to improve my daily life on the whole. I am living as my best self.

What that means for you is this: after reaching the peak, which we talked about in Chapter Seventeen, you are roughly halfway through your journey. You don't transform into the New You the moment you raise your arms and shout, "Yes!" The path down from that high contains some lung-burning peaks of its own – peaks that transform.

You won't find the downhill portion to be smooth sailing. Life will remind you who is boss and check to see how resilient you are and *double*-check what you've learned from the climb. In essence, the most challenging work of the journey is discovering the New You and putting it into practice.

In this chapter, I'll take you through the process of:
- Seeing past the uphills that are thrown at you on the way down. Knowing that you are stronger than you were before you began. Continuing to move, always just taking one step.
- Recognizing how you are now different, separate from the goal itself. You have gotten your degree,

yes – and what kind of person are you now that you have that diploma on your wall? You've opened your business – and what sort of owner will you be?

- Owning that difference, that growth, no matter what anyone else may think or say about it. It's often harder for the people closest to you to accept a change in you than for you to change in the first place.

- Using the New You to begin the next journey, which will now be easier because you have broken out of your comfort zone and flourished in a new one. You know you've got this.

Let's start, as always, with the tools you'll need for this stage.

Tools for Discovering the New You

Tool #1. A certain robustness. This isn't an easy tool to describe. It's not like *Get yourself a sturdy pair of boots and you're good to go.* When we talk about a wine being 'robust', we mean it's full-bodied and rich in flavour. It isn't a quality you achieve by going to the gym. It's an interior thing that comes from:

- The confidence you've gained by reaching the peak of your journey and celebrating it
- The new ability to set a goal, prepare for the path to attain it, overcome fear and stay focused on the pinnacle

- The recognition that you are a unique individual. This richness of spirit is personal to you. No one else has experienced your journey exactly as you have, even if that person was travelling beside you on the same quest. This is about what *you* ponder, save and use.

You don't have to be that person who immediately captures everyone's attention the moment you enter a room. Being robust is not about being bombastic or in command. It is about being assured of your individuality and value. Sometimes the more serene people are the most robust.

Tool #2. A willingness to see life from a different perspective. You would think this would just come naturally after you've seen the world from a new vantage point. That does happen almost automatically at the moment when you're looking out from the peak. But once you're headed back to life as it was before, it can be tempting to scuttle into the old, worn-in place where the limiting beliefs are waiting to take you in again. The willingness to entertain new perspectives comes from:
- Holding on to that new, powerful, moving image of your future that you started when you defined your journey
- Creating a creed for yourself containing, in writing, what you believe now, so that when you find yourself backsliding you can review it and get back on track

- Making a commitment to living by that creed every day. Every. Day. In everything you do.

We'll talk about how to do those things further on in the chapter. What you need right now is merely the willingness to go there.

Tool #3. A set of internal sentences to be used in the face of criticism. And you *will* be criticized, have no doubt about that. Which is why it's important to have responses at the ready, in writing, either to say out loud or simply repeat to yourself. These should be words or sentences that empower you, rather than put you on the defensive or thrust you into an argument. They might sound something like this:

- *I'm sure that makes total sense to you, but it doesn't to me*
- *Thank you, but I'm good*
- *Maybe, but I've got this and every molecule, every cell in my body will help me get there*

Notice that each of those responses contains a "but". Studies have shown that very few people remember what comes before the "but" in the sentence, so you can use that to your advantage. Think about it. If someone says, *I'm really bad at maths but I'm great at English,* your take-away is going to be: *That's the guy who kicks butt when it comes to Dickens.* End your statement with ... robustness.

Keep in mind that often the criticism you face won't come from another person but from inside your own head. It's those voices again, and they aren't going to shut up just because you've done the happy dance at the top of the mountain. They had their say for a long time, so they're going to have to be shown who the New You is. The same sentences you create for other people will work internally – *Thanks for sharing* – *It's working for me* – and the same rule applies: don't defend, don't argue. Just make your statement and move on, never trading in your values.

With those tools in play, you can enter a New Way of Being. This is you, armed to break out of that self-imposed prison for good, making the big decisions, doing the things that are significant for you and not waiting for that 'Special Day' when everything is just right to begin. Today is that Special Day.

Let's look at how to use those tools.

Three Questions for Discovering the New You

Question #1. How are you a different person now that you've achieved success on this journey?

Some of you (and hopefully only a few) will finish reading this book and think, "Nice story," and put it on the pile for the used book shop. Another few may have started using the tips in Part III and, seeing this isn't a quick fix, are skimming for the instant answer that will propel them forward.

More than likely, if you're still reading at this point, you are working through the stages of the journey and already seeing some shifts within you. Now it's time to examine those changes to see what they're telling you.

Let's start with *who you were when you first set out to attain your goal.* Using your journal, try pondering these questions:

- How did you approach a challenge before you engaged in the 'mountain climb'? Did you flee? Resist? Become paralyzed?
- What limiting beliefs and fears clung to you as you started off? Fear of failing? Fear of succeeding? Fear of making a complete fool of yourself?
- What behaviours always held you back? Self-sabotaging? Preferring the couch to action? Listening to naysayers?

As you answer those questions, be aware that there are some things about your former self you will want to keep. Taking this journey does not involve a personality transplant!

- You definitely don't want to give up that sense of humour ... unless making jokes about your own procrastination kept you on the sofa
- Maybe your deep sense of compassion is a keeper ... except when worrying about how everyone you know is going to feel about your goal makes it hard to go for it
- And how about that careful mind that has kept you out of trouble? Has it also kept you out of adventure?

Be sure that what you're clinging to in your former self is not just a security blanket you wrap yourself in. By all means maintain everything about yourself that allows you to step out with confidence. But the climb you've just made has at least suggested some changes. Be willing to recognize them.

With those answers in mind, have a look at *what you immediately notice about yourself now that is different.* Some prompts to get you thinking as you write in your journal:

- Do you feel taller somehow?
- Are you happier to let minor irritations pass?
- Do you find yourself being more confident about, well, most things?
- Are you waking up feeling more positive?
- Are you approaching the day differently?
- Are you more productive?
- Do you find that you are more willing to listen to new ideas? More ready to see the world through the other person's eyes? Keen to know what motivates other people and what holds them back?

You don't have to limit yourself to those prompts. Simply record the newness you see in yourself. And be prepared for it to make a difference. It did for me.

Before the mountain journey, my routine was a frenetic race to get through the day. Up. Showered. Dressed. Soaked in some headlines. Sprinted to the station. Spent an hour on the train reading emails and more news. Got to the office and continued dealing with emails and texts and people popping their heads in, while my own to-do list kept being shoved back. I worked hard, stopping only for a heavy, high-carbohydrate lunch. Then I made the return journey, sometimes via the pub. Got home, collapsed on the sofa and struggled to get motivated to do something. Usually the couch won. Saturdays and Sundays, I just laid in, kicked about, generally didn't do a lot.

Post-Rwenzori, I have changed, and so has the rhythm of my life. I'm up and out of bed at 5.15 a.m. Do a half-hour of posture exercises. After a shower I practise ten minutes of meditation. Cup of high-fat coffee in hand, I leave for work. This start propels me into the day ready for anything.

When I arrive at the office, I greet the team, see how they are, what's happening. Yes, I log on, but immediately crack through some important things on my to-do list before I turn to emails. The bombardment of messages can be overwhelming, so I deal with each one as I'm ready to.

I get as much of my list out of the way as I can, and then I'm ready to tackle requests, the things that are on other people's to-do lists. Every distraction costs you about twenty minutes, so I don't allow them when I'm focusing on the significant tasks of the day. That way I can be present when I'm trying to help someone, rather than ruminating over what I'm not getting done.

A brief lunch break. If I'm heading to exercise after work I will eat, if I'm not then I may just have a small snack or sometimes nothing – intermittent fasting keeps me more tuned for the afternoons. After work I head home, have dinner and then embark on my own continuous improvement. That could be studying, reading, writing, learning something new. Whatever it is, this is my time to focus on what I want to achieve, always taking a step towards my goal.

Before bed, I capture the day in my journal. The good, the interesting, the Oh-that-was-annoying and the how-can-I-do-better points. As I set my alarm, I envision myself getting out of bed the next morning, imagining a big 5.15 a.m. balloon in the air, already knowing what my plan is. That keeps me from hitting the snooze button when 5.15 buzzes. Just like any journey, it starts with prep. My last thoughts as I fall asleep are a verbal summary of what I'm grateful for. This includes all the small things that can easily be overlooked: waking up, health, a family, a roof over my head, food, cash in my pocket.

I wake up the next morning refreshed and ready.

That approach to my day comes from the New Me and the growth mindset that took shape within me after the mountain journey. It took a while to discover it and smooth out the wrinkles. It may, in fact, change, and that I encourage. Every quarter, I check in to see whether it's still working for me, whether I want to add something, alter something, delete something. I couldn't do that if I were the same person I was before.

Whatever new way of living you find yourself wanting to embrace, it is because you are happier, more confident, more positive. You *can* do your life differently. Your rhythm may be very different from mine, especially if you have a family at home or evening obligations to attend to. The point is that you are not the same person, so why would you want to live the same way? Comparing who you were with who you are now gives you the insight you need to modify what hasn't been working for you for a long time.

As you examine this and write it down, you are capturing insights that can get away from you if you only think about them and move on. You'll miss the chance to see them turn into new goals.

That's why I recommend consolidating what you've just journaled about into a Creed. Rather than a direct statement of what you believe, this Creed simply makes clear what you are going to *do* each and every day. Mine is as follows:

Be true to yourself
Help others
Create happiness
Learn one new thing a day
Be dynamic
Take one step to a goal
Be grateful
Give value
Love self and others

Referring to it daily keeps me to the path I want to be on, and yours, whatever it looks like, can do the same for you. Knowing you are living up to that Creed leaves you feeling grateful for all the small achievements, and as we've said before, those small victories laid one on the other are just like the compound interest. Over time, you will reap the rewards.

It will take time and thought to discover yours, but it is all there in your journal. Writing the Creed is merely a matter of putting what you now know into clear, concise form. Give it a go.

Question #2. What do the changes in you mean in your environment as a whole?

Your world isn't necessarily going to change just because YOU have. When I returned from my life-changing experience, it seemed to me the world was completely different. Colours were brighter. Food tasted better. People as a whole were more interesting to me. Naturally, I wanted to talk about that, tell the story of how I came to change, share what I'd gained.

Yeah. And mostly I found out that other people don't really give a monkey's *what* you've accomplished. We talked about this in Chapter Seventeen in terms of your celebration. You may have to honour your achievement by yourself, because the victory is largely interior.

The same holds true for the New You. We can't expect everyone we knew before to stop us in the hall at the office or look at us over a cup of coffee and say, "You know, there is something different about you now. Tell me what's changed." If someone does that, make that person your new best friend. Those kinds of people are rare and wonderful creatures.

It isn't that everyone is simply selfish. If you think about yourself before you made the journey and as you now make your way back, you might not have picked up on shifts in people either. The very experience you've been through and are still going through has altered the way you look at the world. Sure, it's somewhat deflating when nobody else sees it or wants to hear about it. But that's merely your ego shrivelling like yesterday's party balloon. The New You has no such expectations of other people.

Instead, you see your return to 'the real world' as an opportunity to grow even more. You do that by silently responding to every discouraging, disappointing, dismissive situation with this question:

What can I learn here?

Hear me – this doesn't mean don't *feel*. It's important to pay attention to that sinking in your stomach, that torquing of your jaw, that general tensing up that means any minute now you might lash out or run for the hills or just freeze up. Our bodies give us signals that alert us to what we're feeling so we can name it, pause and then respond. And, again, the first response needs to be in your own mind: *What can I learn here? What is this teaching me? What is it that I ultimately need to achieve and how could this help me get there?*

Learning from the rubbish might look something like this:

- Someone you work with comes across as a bully, blustering when he wants his own way and forcing his point until everybody gives in and lets him have it. You know that's not helping, so you may grimace or let him know what you're thinking in a way that doesn't actually change anything. Asking *what can I learn here?*, the New You doesn't alter that opinion – the guy is still a bully – but it changes your response. It's clear that you don't want to become what he is. So instead of reacting, you take the time to respond. Sometimes responding can be silence. Or it can be agreement or a constructive, well-thought-out expression of your opinion at the appropriate time. That's the New You in action.

- Maybe since you've gotten your marketing degree, a vision of starting your own business is driving you. But your spouse or extended family is dead set against it. Why can't you get a job with a corporation? they say. There's security there. Holidays. Sick leave. Suddenly, someone *else's* vision threatens to drive you. You ask yourself: *What can I learn here?* Perhaps it's that if you want to get significant people in your life on board, you're going to have to have a solid plan, backed up by financial figures. You put up a flip chart and get started.

- Sitting at the head of the table with those who now work for you because you've gotten that promotion, you want to put your vision for the department before them. The minute you open the PowerPoint presentation, the heads begin to shake, and the comments are hurled at you. *We tried that once, and it didn't pan out. You'll never get that past the higher-ups. This looks like it's going to be more work for us.* It's like they're building a wall around you. New person that you are, you ask yourself: *What can I learn here?* Huh. This all sounds familiar. You used to react the way they're doing right now, back before you faced your fears head-on and saw them for what they were. Maybe the process you went through could help your people get past the things that are holding them back as a team. Out comes a flip chart. You make a plan. New You is functioning well.

- Somewhere on your journey, you developed a great relationship with another person. It's honest and supportive, and now the New You wants all your relationships to be that way. You invite your friends and family members out one by one for coffee or a beer and try being authentic, try asking how they're doing and offering positive input. And one by one they look at you blankly and then go back to whatever it was the two of you used to do before – gossiping, complaining, bashing other people. This isn't going well. So the New You asks: *What can I learn here?* That could be that this is not how you see yourself. This is not helping you be the difference you want to be. The New You remembers that you will be the average of the persons you spend the most time with, and you need to choose wisely.

That last example brings us to an important point. As a new person, you may not be able to fit into that old environment any more. You may indeed need new friends. A different job. Even a fresh place to live. If where you are in your life is no longer congruent with who you are now, that could define a new journey. Which brings us to our third question.

Question #3. How will this change in you affect your next journey?

Before we go there, be sure you understand this part: if you're beginning to realize that the New You would fit in better in a different job or another city, while there is something to be said for marching into the boss's office and resigning, unless you have no commitments – no spouse, family, contract or debt – it's advisable to prepare for and define your new path while you stay where you are for the time being. Otherwise, broken promises and legal obligations will hinder your forward movement. Keep the old and the new in parallel until you're ready to make the leap.

Of course, if you are completely untethered, you may very well walk out of that dead-end job and just head for Phase One of your new mountain. But who has a life that's totally unconnected with anyone else's? That doesn't mean wait until everybody's on board before you decide to make a change. Just calculate the possible losses carefully.

In either case, or even if your next journey doesn't involve a drastic change in your current situation, you'll still need to define that next thing the same way you have for the one you're now completing. And prepare for it. And face the accompanying fears, which may be different from the ones you encountered last time. What's different now is you.

Who you are now will make this new adventure easier in some ways. You know how it's done. You know some of what to expect. You are more confident. More open. Other changes will be unique to you, so look at what you wrote in your journal for Questions 1 and 2. The possibilities are virtually endless. Here are a few:

- You've found your true voice, or you're beginning to
- You've realized you're far more creative than you thought you were
- You have more energy because you're spending less time in couch potato mode
- Some health issues have resolved themselves
- You're naturally commanding a little more respect
- You're less socially anxious
- You're more comfortable being alone

How does that affect your choice of a new journey?

Let's say you've discovered you're more creative than you used to be. That could mean that instead of going for the next level in the design business you work for, you begin to plan the creating and selling of your own line of clothes, day planners, tennis rackets, whatever.

Or you've found your true voice. Might that call for at least dipping your toe into doing presentations or podcasts, rather than simply blogging or putting together newsletters?

How about the fact that you're now more comfortable being alone? What if that is nudging you to get out of the four-roommates-in-the-same-flat situation and start planning for your own digs?

As you read and study what you've written about the New You and ideas spring from there, write them down. If one of them won't leave you alone, journal about it some more, brainstorm, until it's time for a flip chart.

Whether what you see as your next mountain is a gentle hill – you're going to change your look to match your aspirations or you plan to reorganize your home work space so you can start that novel – or it's a Mount Everest life change like switching careers or leaving a toxic relationship – choosing the right one depends on your understanding of your new self.

As you ask yourself *Is this the right path? Am I ready?* use your sense of who you are now as your guide.

If you're finding your true voice and you want to do presentations, but you're not quite sure you have the skills, let the next journey be toward developing those skills – taking a public speaking course, getting a coach, practising in front of small groups.

If you realize you're stronger than you knew and you're considering leaving that unhealthy relationship, but you're still questioning whether you've given it all you have, perhaps the next journey's goal is to be sure. See a counsellor. Write down what you want in a relationship and test whether it can happen.

Here's the deal: you are constantly on a journey. It isn't so much what the goal itself is – it's about having a clear one. That's something you've learned from a past of flatlining your way through life with no particular end-game in mind.

And it's not so much whether the mountain is a rolling hill or the highest point in your personal mountain range. It's how you approach that journey. Every goal you set, every new path you decide on, every peak you want to reach, will call for the same phases you've just been through and are now completing. It will be easier this time because you are an experienced climber.

Yet at the same time, it could be harder. Because of your heightened confidence and your developing interaction skills and whatever other positive qualities are now taking shape in you, you'll find yourself picking bigger tasks. Pulling a little farther from limiting beliefs and people, who will try to haul you back. Wanting to be far more than you are now. While some of the peaks you'll have to summit to get to those mountains may be small ones, the ultimate climbs will inevitably be more challenging simply because of their magnitude.

The New You can do it.

That doesn't mean every path you set out on is now going to reach the summit if you just follow the structure. Life sometimes intervenes. Take my youngest daughter. She'd dreamed of working for the airlines for years. Once she was old enough, she set her sights on British Airways and began the prep part of her journey. She knew what she had to do and worked hard at it. The peak was being selected for their training programme. She was chosen. And there she was, ready to become a new person ...

And the COVID-19 pandemic shut it all down. She was properly prepared, she'd done everything right, but the training was put on hold indefinitely. The rug had been pulled out from under her, and she was headed for the floor.

"Upset" doesn't begin to describe the state she was in. She had already given notice on her current job, and she had the pressure of bills to pay. Hopes dashed, it felt to her like the end of the world. In a sense it was, since she had put all her eggs of happiness into that one basket. This beautiful, caring young woman who just wanted to serve in the skies was reduced to tears.

Remember the poem about dads? "A dad is someone who wants to catch you before you fall." Although I was immensely proud of what she had achieved, I couldn't catch her this time. I let the tears pass, gave her a sleep or two. And then we chatted.

We talked about the need for a new journey, perhaps a smaller one. Sure, she had the option of sitting and doing nothing and waiting for someone else to sort it. But that isn't a journey, and I wasn't seeing a goal in there. The better option, she agreed, was to realize that the British Airways journey still existed; it had merely been postponed. Could she use this time to be even better prepared for it? She needed a temporary job to pay those bills, but could that be something that would employ the skills she'd gained while getting herself ready for BA selection?

The key was to begin a small but forward-moving journey that would get her back on a path and out of the rut of fear and anxiety and desperation. She can still focus on the British Airways summit; there are simply other peaks to reach between here and there.

She went back to her old employer and rescinded her resignation. Then she set herself three new goals: learn a language, get fit and learn more first aid skills. She was flexible. She adjusted. She found the solution in a new journey, and now each day she does something that will take her up and over the new hills, knowing that the BA training programme still exists in her future.

And who knows where these new visions will take her? That's the beauty of life. It just happens, and maybe BA will unfold or perhaps one of these new visions will turn into something she hasn't even considered. But she's doing something. She's taking a step.

My daughter is at the *beginning* of her working life. What about the other end, the person who is retiring?

It's common for someone facing the end of a role that's been his or hers for decades to fall into thinking:

I used to be a _____. *I was a* _____. *I don't know who I am now.* Those statements in themselves bring about fear – of emptiness, of unfamiliar (or no) routines or of losing identity. These proclamations are not dynamic; they don't allow for change. They are caught-in-the past statements. It is fine not to lose sight of experience and accomplishments, but when someone asks us about ourselves, we don't start at the beginning with, *I **was** a college student* or *I **was** a trainee.* Yeah great, but what are you now?

If looked at as the next journey, retirement should really call forth some productive questions:

- *Who am I as a result of all those years of reaching peaks?*
- *How can I apply those amazing qualities in a new life?*
- *What have I always wanted to do but didn't have time for or refused to believe I could?*

In fact, why not abandon the word 'retirement' completely? Why not think of it as a beginning? The start of a fresh journey. A time to find a new passion and train for it. Fine-tune it. Overcome the fears attached to it. Reach the summit and celebrate. Become even *more* than the awesome person you already are after all your years of service to the working world.

If you can't escape the has-been connotations of the word 'retirement', reframe it as just a date. Pass it by like any other day (unless you do want to celebrate it as a peak). Then get on with being a human who still requires social interaction, change and balance, a person who will need developing in ways you couldn't even think about when you were working forty-plus hours a week.

What if you don't know what you want to do next? Just become involved in something you love, simply for the pure enjoyment of it. That's allowed, you know. Staying active with something positive – both mentally and physically – allows you to see new opportunities and be open to them. You may end up with a very different problem: *there are so many, I don't know which one to focus on!* The 'problem' of abundance is an enviable challenge.

Action

As you become this New You, be sure that you:

- Have developed a healthy routine, especially for starting your day
- Have written a Creed to carry with you
- Are learning from the difficult situations and setbacks
- Are using what you've learned about You to begin to define your next journey

Time to Move On to the Next Phase?

You don't have to wait until you feel *There, Perfect, Fully Transformed* before you move ahead to the next phase of *this* journey. Nobody ever completely reaches those descriptions. The New You will continue to develop for the rest of your life, as long as you are always consciously growing. Which means there are no absolute markers that determine that you are now New.

There are some indicators, though. As always, they'll look somewhat different for every person because we're all unique, but in general you'll know that Newness is happening when:

- You deviate off your path *and* you realize it. Before, you probably stumbled around a lot and never actually knew you were stumbling because you didn't *have* a path. When it's clearly defined, it doesn't take long to recognize when you're not on it. The New You has a think: *where am I on that journey and what is it I can do to get me back on track?*

- You don't feel congruent with what you're doing. Perhaps in the past you could go along with whatever life tossed at you, or you bit the bullet and ground through it, or you felt desperate and drank a six-pack. If you find yourself out of sorts, you can see that what's happening isn't working for you *and* you look at how you can change that, the New You is at work.

- The day doesn't feel like it's flowing *and* you pause to determine whether there's an external cause (somebody's out sick and you have to do her job or the internet went down just when you were trying to finish up a report that's due) or an internal one (you got up late or you skipped meditation or a limiting belief is nagging at you). The old you goes down the drain with it. Day wasted. The New You remembers what's New, applies it to the moment and literally saves the day.

On the mountain, we had to pause on more than one occasion to assess why things weren't going well and what we could do about it. Should we wait an hour to see if the weather would change? Should we leave our friend to rest or stay with him? Even on that icy glacier when I was sure I was going to die, I had to look at where I was and what I had waiting for me elsewhere. This doesn't only happen on a literal mountain. It happens in life. All. The. Time.

When that happens, if you are a New You, you deal with that far differently now.

The New You who wakes up late does an abbreviated version of the routine instead of slipping back into hectic hell. You know you'll get back into rhythm tomorrow.

The New You who gets pulled off the path onto someone else's steep, bumpy, unpaved road says, *They have their journey, I have mine,* and quietly returns to it.

The New You who is having an out-of-sorts day reviews his or her Creed or checks out that flip chart or writes in the journal. The way becomes clear and the mood sorts itself.

The New You is now ready to leave a legacy.

CHAPTER NINETEEN
LEAVING A LEGACY

WHEN I LEFT THE RWENZORI BEHIND, I would have been happy never to see that mountain range, or any other, again. Ever.

A piece of me had died on Mount Stanley – a piece I will never recover. I'm not sure I want it back. What's important is what I gained: the New Me we talked about in our last chapter. I want to retain that, and I've reshaped my life so I can.

But I don't just want to hold on to it. I want to pass it on as well.

That first evening after we'd made our final our descent, Michiel, Jake, George and I went out in search of food and drink, and as I've recounted in Chapter Thirteen, I took my diary notebook with me, the school exercise book where I captured my thoughts – and my turmoil – from day one of the climb to the end. At this point it was a ragtag affair, and the handwriting had disintegrated into near illegibility as the days passed. I didn't want to relive any of it that night. It was still too raw and sensitive.

Still I took it with me, and I left the guys to go in search of something different from what they were going to eat. After a bit of negotiation, I secured some barbecue and, while it was prepared, I strolled down the street and watched a large, gangly marabou stork forage for *his* dinner in a rubbish bin. I could totally relate. Too tired to go far, I sat down and just held the notebook in my hands. As I looked at the tattered thing with its almost unintelligible scratchings of ink, I asked myself the question: *So what?* Did it matter that I had everything written down? What was I going to do with it?

I could just stick it away somewhere and realize at a future date that I'd misplaced it.

Or I could be a little more aggressive and burn it before anyone read – as if they could – how close to breaking I'd come.

The more I considered it, both then and later, the more I was convinced that I could neither forget about it nor destroy it. In those pages was an opportunity. A chance to stitch together the trauma of a terror attack, the emotions of being near death on a number of levels and the phases of the life-changing mountain climb. More than that, it was an opening for sharing a story that just might help other people. A story of vulnerability, the *power* of being vulnerable – vulnerable enough to change your life.

What if I took what was in that journal and used it as the basis for a book? Not just another Look At Me, I Climbed a Mountain volume. Other people have reached higher physical peaks and suffered more trauma and written about it. This would be a book about how to take a journey – any real-life journey. That's what I learned from the climb, and that was what I had to share.

You have now been on that journey with me and hopefully you are on your own upward path as we speak. I like to think you're discovering a New You. Now it's time to consider what that New You might leave with the world. Just as I did when I held my worse-for-wear notebook in my hand and saw the potential, you can look at your journey as recounted in your journal and discover the legacy that can arise from it.

For me, a legacy isn't about what I will leave behind once I've died. Sure, I hope my book is still on the shelves after I depart this earthly frame. My daughters would enjoy the royalties. I also have a dream that my presentations will still exist on YouTube and other venues long after my funeral. But my real idea of a legacy is what I can share *now*, so that the journey isn't just about me.

Before you protest that you aren't legacy-leaving material, know that I am a massive believer that everyone is amazing. Everyone. And the only thing stopping us from creating a legacy is our own thoughts. If you remember anything from this story and the guidelines here in Part III, let it be that.

Besides, we're not talking about everybody writing a book, making a documentary, founding a non-profit organization or starting a movement. You *can* do that, but if that isn't what calls to you, a legacy is still part of the journey. Sometimes the seemingly smallest lessons from that journey are the ones most worth passing on. What you learned could:

- Comfort someone who feels alone on their path, because you've been there.
- Give someone the confidence to move forward, because you've been stuck yourself.
- Model vulnerability to someone who has always been afraid of it, because they're watching you.
- Share just that one part of the puzzle that's missing for someone, because you know where to find lost pieces.

While leaving a legacy of any kind is altruistic at its core, and you do it without the expectation that you will get anything back, it will also give *you* meaning. As hard as you try to be selfless in sharing what you now know, you'll still gain personal satisfaction and a deeper sense of happiness.

How you discover your legacy and what to do with it when you do find it is what this chapter is about. We'll walk through legacies you've left – and there *have* been some, whether you realize it or not. We'll figure out what you have to share, what you can do to make your journey even more worth taking. And we'll get you started on ensuring that legacy. It's a mini-journey in itself.

Let's start, as always, by gathering the tools you'll need for this phase.

Tools You'll Need For Leaving a Legacy

Tool #1: Confidence in your new knowledge

This one is especially important if you've ever thought of yourself in any of these ways:

- "I'm not a leader. I'm way more comfortable being on the support team."
- "I'm not perfect so I don't have any business telling other people what I know. I'd feel like a fraud."
- "Nobody really listens to me. I'm just not that impressive."
- If you've been paying attention throughout this book, especially here in Part III, you'll recognize those as self-limiting beliefs. They may have come from a thousand reinforcements during your childhood and bad experiences in your teen and young adult years which took such firm root in you that you started to believe them and still do.
- Except that now you are a New You. You have reached a peak and examined who you are now. That completely qualifies you to leave a treasure trove of what you know that can help someone else who engages in that same stifling self-talk. It starts with letting those thoughts pass straight through your mind while you return to the person you now find yourself to be. That person thinks:
- "I have led myself to my goal. That makes me a leader. Period."

- "I don't have to be perfect. No one is. It's the wise leader who admits that – and I am that wise leader."
- "I didn't used to have that much of importance to say. Now I do. If I speak with quiet confidence and what I say is meaningful, people will hear me. I have found my voice."

That is confidence.

Tool #2: An understanding of the qualities a leaver of legacies has.

No matter what your personality type, you can develop the following traits that make you accessible. That encourage people to hear and trust you. That make you the real deal.

- **Vulnerability.** Just as I have had to own the points of weakness I struggled with on the mountain climb and in the aftermath of the terrorist attack, you will need to be able to share yours. The telling of your *whole* story makes it real and reassures people that they don't have to start off as the person they're going to become. We all tend to trust an individual who has risen to a peak through hard work and mistakes they've learned from – far more than we do someone who refuses to admit it was ever difficult. At that point, we shrug and say, "I can never do that, so why try?"
- **Patience.** You're jazzed about your newfound knowledge and the changes that have taken place

inside you. It's tempting to lay it all out for people and expect them to embrace it and change just as you did. But *your* legacy doesn't constitute *their* journey. You can only make the information and concepts available. What people do with that is up to them. Be happy to let them find their way and be on standby should they come to you for help.

- **Self-Awareness.** Have you ever been driven practically out of your mind by someone who has quit smoking and not only wants to recount every detail of his victory but tries to shame, bully and cajole anyone with a cigarette in her hand to follow his lead and be healed? If you don't already smoke, this guy makes you want to light up immediately. We can't foster change in those who don't want to change. We can't push our legacy on people. First of all, it doesn't work that way (as you'll see below). Secondly, it's annoying, so you quickly lose your audience and any influence you may have had. And finally, it destroys your credibility. You really can't help people become quietly confident when you are dominating the conversation like a politician running for office. No need to be an obnoxious salesman. Which leads us to ...

- **Authenticity.** The opposite of this is hypocrisy. If you aren't walking the talk, practising what you're preaching, being a living example of the very thing you're trying to share, you will be completely ineffective. Think of an obese person leading a weight loss seminar and you'll get the idea. Again, you don't have to be perfect. But you do need to be visibly living the life whose qualities you're trying to pass on. That means staying on your current path. Frequently reviewing where you are to keep yourself going in the right direction. Practising a daily rhythm that allows you to be your best self at any given moment.

- **A Listening Mindset.** Leaving a legacy isn't just about talking to people, presenting what you know, telling folks how they can change their lives. In fact, the greater part of a legacy is action rather than words. To achieve that, we all need to learn to listen far better than we probably do. We are actually built for it: we have two ears and only one mouth. That means we would do well to listen twice as much as we speak.

Take as much time as you need with your journal to think about, examine and explore these two tools and the five traits. If there are some you know you haven't mastered yet, make that a side trip on your journey. Developing them is the prep phase of leaving a legacy. And as you know by now, preparation is absolutely key.

When you feel ready to delve more deeply into what you might pass on and how, spend some time with the Three Questions.

Three Questions for Leaving a Legacy

Question 1. What in your life has already created a legacy?

If your first thought is "I have never left a legacy," think again. We have all passed on ideas, experiences, skills – many times without knowing it. In fact, the legacies we've left may not even be the ones we intended.

Several years ago, I had the brilliant idea of starting a bouncy castle business. You know what I'm talking about, right? Those huge inflatable things that look like castles which kids enter and bounce on until they throw up.

I pulled in a friend of mine who had just been declared redundant in a long-standing job. For him, redundancy felt like a terrible death and divorce all rolled into one. He had put his life and soul into that company only to be told, "Thank you, but you're no longer necessary."

He'd already had a brilliant go at starting his own franchises in things he was interested in, but nothing really gave him that va va voom, so he ended up being a stay-at-home dad. I thought *Lucky him.* But he was the man, the breadwinner. That wasn't completely satisfying for him.

Fast forward to my crazy bouncy castle idea. We injected some cash and got to researching types of castles and designing our own, finding the best supplier, the best material, the safety standards, the insurance. We produced two amazing bouncy castles. They were our babies. Such impressive bits of kit.

We had created a new business. He'd brought lots of business acumen to the party, and I brought ideas and proactivity. I had no idea about most of the business side, spreadsheets and details, but he did, and I provided the practical impact. We advertised, we scooped up some business and we did it. The bouncy castle business was off.

Now, those things were heavy. It was hard work but what a good time we had shifting them around to different parties and seeing the kids' faces as they shouted, "The bouncy castle man is here!" That brought as much joy to us as it did them.

But the fun drew to a close. I was going to work overseas, and my mate and his wife had decided to start their own events business. A natural path and a natural conclusion. I sold the castles for a small loss overall.

Over a beer or two a few years later he said, "Jonny, that bouncy castle business really gave me the mojo to make something of my life. That was the pivot point that turned me around." He told me it gave him a real purpose and a reason to be at a very difficult place in his life. He thanked me and still does for giving him that opportunity.

For me it was great fun, we learned a lot and had a laugh shifting those bulky bits of kit around. But him getting his mojo back was for me an unexpected by-product of this small venture. Who cares that we lost money? There was a far better legacy, as he and his wife went on to create an awesome events business together.

If you're still at a loss for a legacy, try walking through the process below. And please do it. It's important for you to realize that you can pass on something lasting, because you've done it before.

Ponder these in your journal.

1. Ask some people who are close to you: *Have I positively influenced you in any way?* A few cautions here. One, ask people you are on good terms with. Anyone with a grudge will use this opportunity to berate you for all the negative influences you have bestowed – real and imagined. Two, be sure to use the word *positively,* for the same reason. Even loved ones who appreciate you can see this as an opening to give an all-encompassing assessment. And three, frame the question just that way. Not *How have I,* but *Have I.* That way, if the answer is, "Well, no, you haven't," the conversation can be over. Try somebody else!

2. Think back over your life and ferret out a season that was particularly good – not just for you but for one or more other people as well. What part did you play in the goodness of that season? Were those other people affected in a positive way that lasted? You didn't necessarily have to do anything consciously. Maybe it was just you being you that encouraged, strengthened or consoled someone else.

3. Review conversations from your past. Has anyone ever come to you and thanked you for something you've shown them, even if you didn't know it at

313

the time? Has someone told you that something you did affected them in a healthy way? It can be hard to uncover those moments because we spend so much time thinking about our mistakes and cringing over past shame. But let those compliments rise to the surface of your memory.

Look at what you've written down and allow it to shape a list of the legacies you've already left in your life. None is too small to mention. Some examples might help.

- Years ago, you let go of your family of origin's narrow view of cultural differences and had the courage to travel and explore. Your younger sister saw that, and when she was of age, she asked you for advice on how to start seeing the world. That's a legacy.

- The season when you were at university was awesome for you. The freedom, the study, the life-learning … you wished it would never end. And a lot of that was because you had peers who were doing the same thing. There was a sense of working toward common goals. You always seemed to be the one who formed a study group. Planned a day trip for everybody. Reflected out loud how much you were all changing. Some of those people came out of that season different than they would have without you. That's a legacy.

- Not long ago, you ran into a former student in a cafe. She had tears in her eyes when she thanked you for not letting her slide in her work in your class. She said your constant vigilance over her has made all the difference in her work ethic. That, too, is a legacy.

Now have another think, this time about the qualities in yourself that allowed you to pass on those good things – even before you became the New You. That list might include things like courage, positivity, determination, compassion – and maybe even plain old stubbornness. You haven't lost those qualities, and, coupled with the fresh ones you've discovered in your current journey, they make you infinitely qualified to have an influence.

So what do you do now? You go on to Question 2.

Question 2: What do you see as the legacy you could now leave as a result of your journey?
Before I began writing this book, I collated my thoughts. Then I found opportunities to speak to people in groups, people I didn't know, and told them my story and what I learned from it. Many of those listening came to me in person or via email to express how motivating that was, and how in the future they would use the Phases of the Mountain. In the year since then, I've given a number of presentations, and every time the response is similar. Some come back to me months later and tell me that when they're facing any kind of difficulty, they can locate where they are on the mountain and determine how to move forward from there.

My legacy was beginning.

As I've stated earlier, not everyone will start a speaking career or write a book or do anything else quite so public. Determining what *you* can pass on requires awareness, not just of the things you've learned from your journey but of yourself. These questions may be helpful in discovering this last phase.

1. What *concrete things* do you now know that you didn't before you started your climb? In my case, that had to do with the proper kit. Living in the misery of wet, cold clothes wasn't lost on me, and I don't want anyone else to suffer unnecessarily on a trek. People really can learn from others' mistakes. Think in practical, physical terms and see what you come up with. It's the easiest place to start.

2. We've already talked at length about the *interior things* you've learned. That's the New You covered in Chapter Eighteen. Which of those mental, emotional or spiritual lessons seems the most powerful to you? Things like finding your voice, learning the value of humility or discovering that vulnerability is not weakness are what we're talking about here. Consider what truly has changed your life already.

3. Could that lesson you've chosen be *valuable to someone else?* What young woman in her early twenties doesn't long to find her voice? What boss whose employees are unresponsive couldn't benefit from learning the value of humility? What guy who has a string of failed relationships behind him wouldn't do well to learn that vulnerability isn't weakness? Notice that we're being very specific

here. Even though I'd like to think my legacy could be beneficial to anybody, in reality my audience consists of people who already have a longing for a better, more satisfying life.

4. What might sharing that concrete information or that invaluable lesson with that specific group of people look like? Let your imagination kick in. Brainstorm for the possibilities. I've encouraged you to dream big, so do that, keeping in mind that you'll break this down into phases – because this is the start of a new journey. For example, you might say ...

- I could start by helping my timid young adult niece find her voice. That could lead to working with her and a small group of her friends. Which could develop into a blog or the use of Instagram. After that, who knows?

- I could create a meme about humility in the workplace, turn it into a poster, hang it up in my office, the conference room, above the coffee machine. Somebody is sure to ask about it, which could lead to a training curriculum. I don't even have to be the one to teach it. But I might.

- I could take a group of relationship-weary guys on an overnight hike and create an atmosphere for them to open up. That could lead to me sharing what I now know about vulnerability with partners. If it goes somewhere beyond that, great, but those guys will at least have a chance in their future relationships.

As you can see, legacies can start with something seemingly small. They may broaden, they may not. But even that first step counts.

If all of that still seems daunting, think about this: you can leave a legacy for yourself. That isn't selfish, self-absorbed, self-serving, self-centred or any of the other adjectives that give 'self' a bad name. If we don't nurture what we've begun in our new selves, that newness won't last. And if we do, the opportunities for leaving legacies will eventually appear. Let me share an example from my own experience.

After the mountain journey, I made some significant changes in myself (as I've described), and one of those was the pursuit of a larger sense of well-being. That began during a Tony Robbins event, where just outside the auditorium I discovered a kiosk where someone was demonstrating the Egoscue Method of posture therapy. I thought *What's this about?* as I had never heard of it. I had a quick chat with the representative about the functions of the form of the body. When the muscular-skeletal parts are not working as they should, the body's organs can't operate at an optimum level. Once the muscular and skeletal parts are properly functioning, the inner systems can as well. In turn this means the person is no longer wrestling with the aches and pains of an out-of-whack body and mind. It was all based on the role of posture.

As soon as I learned about this link between posture and overall mental and physical health, I made it a journey to improve mine. After sending off four pictures for assessment, one for the front, the back, and both sides, I received feedback and a series of really simple exercises designed specifically to put my body back into shape. No weights were involved; it was just me and a few stretches and small actions. I committed to this every day and, after a very short time, I noticed the benefits. The pain reduced, I slept better and no longer did I get knots in my shoulders. It was great.

But that wasn't enough. The results were so profound, I felt a legacy coming on. Eager to help other people have that same positive experience, I signed up for a course, received online instruction over six months and completed the required hands-on experience. I now have my certification as a Posture Alignment Therapist.

I didn't see this in my future when I was preparing for the mountain climb. New goals – and their accompanying legacies – appear as long as we continue to grow along the path. And as long as we keep asking, *What have I learned? Why is this important to me? How can I make it deeper and richer?*

I hope that at this point you have at least a glimmer of what you might pass on and how. If not, continue journaling about it, brainstorming, paying attention during your day to where people are listening to you, what questions they're asking. It will come to you.

In any case, go ahead with Question 3. You may be surprised at how ready you are.

Question 3: What is the first step you can take in ensuring your legacy?

If I had told any of my former English teachers that I was planning to write a book, I would have been met with shrieks of hysteria. In some cases, a stroke might have been triggered. Putting words on paper in any coherent form had never been my strong suit, to say the least.

Yet this book was part of the legacy I longed to leave, and I had to at least give it a go. I clearly needed a writing mentor to guide me through the process, but where to turn? Seemingly out of the blue, an old contact who knew what I wanted to do said, "I've met an amazing lady – let me introduce you." Even as I met her, heard about what she had to offer and what working together might look like, I still heard the fear voices saying, *The story's not profound enough. No one will want to hear about it, much less read it.*

But I knew enough to take Step One. Procuring her services was that step. And here we are.

Action

There will be as many Step Ones as there are those of you taking this journey. Each is specific to the legacy you want to leave. Some guidelines to discovering that first move may prove helpful.

- Figure out what you *don't* know or don't have that you'll need to shape this legacy. I lacked writing skills. For you, a bit more fitness might be required to give you the stamina for this part of the journey. Or a public speaking class. Or a bit more capital.

Think of these as gaps that need to be filled to get things wholly ready.

- Make a list of questions you need to have answered. These aren't knowledge- or skill-related but apply to your intended recipients. What do they need? Where are they now? What would make this easier for them? What do their inner voices sound like? Any actor, speaker, writer or presenter will tell you how essential it is to know your audience. It's vital for leaving a legacy as well.

- Prioritize those need-to-knows in order of importance for moving forward with this. That item at the top of your list is your Step One.

If you have come this far in discovering and planning your legacy, you *know* this thing you are about to do for other people is important. It has merit. And if you have truly dug deep in the preceding chapters of Part III, you also know that you can do this. Take that first step, and then the next, and then the next – just as you have done all along this journey.

Let me send you off on the path with some final thoughts on legacy-leaving.

One, a legacy *can* be simply cash and assets we leave as we pass on. There's a good chance that will have a positive effect on your heirs. But that benefits them in only one way, and it doesn't have the potential for being far-reaching like the kinds of legacies we've been talking about. Why wait until you are gone to leave something

ONE MOUNTAIN, TWO MINDS

when you can participate in the growth of this inheritance? In that case, everybody wins.

Two, check your motivation. If there is any small gleam of you trying to impress people with what you now know or the slightest glint of you simply doing this so people won't think you're selfish – deal with that before you even begin. The only way a legacy such as this lasts and multiplies is if you genuinely have the best interests of other people as your basic reason for doing it. And not just what you *think* would serve them best, but what you have discovered they truly need. Have some brutally honest conversations with yourself. Resolve what you have to.

Three, allow this good thing you are doing to motivate you to take even more life-giving journeys. I'll share a personal story.

In mid-2017, a friend took me with him to a local orphanage here in Nairobi. Not my typical hang-out spot, but I was keen to give something back, so I went along and quickly found myself taking the kids swimming – more like preventative drowning as they all jumped in without a care only to realize simple floating had not been mastered. Still, I immediately knew this was something I could do. And there was more. Gradually I became more involved, buying them food, spending Christmas Day with them. Many had had such terrible starts, everything from burns to drug abuse to serious assaults. Each carried his or her life in a small box, and they'd all lived like acrobats as they bounced from place to place. For some, home had been a discarded car tyre propped against a pile of bricks. Yet every one of them carried on with joy, no matter what their backstory.

I wanted to do something more for them. I had a deep desire for them to know they were loved, that they weren't just forgotten souls destined for life on the harsh streets.

Enter the New Me.

Until my own journey, I wouldn't have been able to spend time this way. My mindset closed off such opportunities. In fact, I always thought what I was doing was correct, that my approach was the only way. I hadn't figured out why my journeys were so difficult, why I always reached the rut of fear and slid back down to the beginning. I never would have walked into that orphanage.

One of the most limiting parts of that mindset was my hang-up with money. I was always told as a kid that there wasn't enough. When I got older, had a family, went through a divorce, I felt like I was a cash machine that no one needed a PIN number for. Cash flow only went one way – out – and I was spiralling into debt.

The New Me became aware that this whole life approach was not working. As I began to look upon things differently as the result of my journey, I found myself treasuring the important things in life. Being in a different country, in a culture outside my comfort zone showed me what I had in common with all other human beings, and what we shared was the need for those important things – love, compassion, belonging, self-worth. As a result, my attitude toward finances changed. Giving without expectation of return actually became rewarding.

I did some things to stop the constant drain on my monetary resources. That allowed me to do more than spend time with the orphans – valuable as that was. My first step in this new legacy was to buy them textbooks. Next, I was able to pay for two brothers – Jonny and Brian – to go to school. The joy on their faces, knowing that someone appreciated who they were and believed in them, made my tear ducts work overtime.

They are also on a journey. They have a summit. They will one day be successful. They will learn to forgive those who abandoned or abused them. And one day they will pass all of this on to others who are where they were. Teaching them this may be the most important legacy of all.

The ongoing benefits of that first step you take cannot be fathomed. You may never know what all of them are. But you *will* know that there will be more journeys to come for you. Leaving a legacy becomes part of who you are now: a person of warmth and kindness who finds out what's truly important and makes a dream come true for someone else.

Time to Move On to the Next Phase?

Wait! Isn't this the last phase? Aren't we done?

You already know the answer to that question: we are never done when it comes to growing, developing and sharing value with other people. Planning your legacy simply brings you back to the beginning as you do the Prep and then Define and Map the Journey, Face the

Fears, Reach the Peak and Celebrate. The New You can't rest on the proverbial laurels.

This is not about climbing that corporate ladder, becoming greedy for additional wealth or gaining more and more power and status. This is about living a more meaningful life in a rhythm that makes you increasingly authentic and serves other people in real ways.

So how do you know you're ready to move on to the next journey?

If you've been doing the work on this chapter, you have at least an inkling of what that is. If you've discovered the ever-evolving New You, you probably already have ideas for journeys beyond the legacy.

Yet there are still more clues. You are ready if:

- You no longer feel imprisoned by self-limiting thoughts. You know where the key is, and you're using it on a daily basis. Time to go for it.
- You aren't put off by people who say things like *Why do you want to help people? What's in it for you? This can't be done. You've gotten crazy lately. Things are just fine the way they are; why try to change it?* You know that if babies gave up on learning to walk, we would all be crawling. That kind of ridicule can be wearing, but if it doesn't matter on a deep level, if what you want to do is congruent with your values, your own personal vision and mission, you are ready.
- The idea of doing your level best is energizing, rather than daunting. You don't long to just camp out on the couch. You don't get tired even think-

ing about putting forth the effort. You're no longer content to furnish the rut you've been living in, because you know the rut is not where you belong. It's not where *anyone* belongs. If you are excited in whatever way enthusiasm and motivation feels like to you, it is time to begin that next journey.

As for me, the joy I receive from sharing the pain, the misery and the growth of this period of my life have spurred me on to the next right thing. I'm in the process of creating a diary of sorts which walks future readers through the phases of the journey and provides a journal. The flip chart is on the wall.

The feedback from those I reach out to is my motivation.

They are releasing themselves from their own prisons.

They are getting on with a new journey in a measured way.

They are conquering summits.

They are going on to do amazing things.

Why wouldn't I continue having journeys?

More importantly ... why wouldn't you?

ABOUT THE AUTHOR

 Internationally commended coun-terterrorism veteran Jonathan Mearns is a father of two daughters and a loyal son, brother, and uncle. He is also a goodwill Ambassador to a children's charity in Kenya: Imma-nuel Afrika, who focus on rescuing and rehabilitating children from the Nairobi streets.

Jonathan has a passion for adventure, self-educa-tion, and entrepreneurship which includes co-found-ing London Christmas Tree Rental and Holly Berry Trees.

For more information visit:
www.jonathanmearns.com

Printed in Great Britain
by Amazon